Helping Kids Rise and Shine

A Tapping Guidebook for Stress, Anxiety, and Bullying

Empowering Parents, Teachers, and Caring Adults

Paul Boulton

Copyright © 2025 Paul Boulton
All Rights Reserved Without Prejudice Ab initio.

No part of this publication may be reproduced in whole or in part, stored in a retrievable system, or transmitted in any form or by any means, electronic, mechanical, photocopying, recording or otherwise, without written permission of the copyright holder.

ISBN: 978-0-9944827-8-5 (Print)
ISBN: 978-1-7640673-3-1 (ePub)
ISBN: 978-1-7640673-0-0 (PDF)
FIRST PUBLISHED 2025

Published by: Boulton Books
Sunshine Coast, Queensland, Australia

Cover design: HMD Publishing
Cover photography: iStock/Pixdeluxe
Internal book design: Shahid Aziz, shahidaziz59@gmail.com
Research, compilation and development: Elaine Gentles
Illustrations: Sarbani Sarkar, Iconfield, and Wayne Knetter*
Diagrams: Elaine Gentles*
(* Based upon the tapping procedures of Dr. Roger Callahan and Gary Craig)

For more information:
www.helpingkidsriseandshine.com
www.facebook.com/HelpingKidsRiseandShine
www.boultonbooks.com.au
www.paulboulton.com.au

This book presents the insights and experiences of the author, Paul Boulton. It introduces the techniques and concepts associated with Targeted Energy Focused Tapping (Targeted EFT) and provides readers with a tool that when used with children, can support their well-being. It is not intended to replace medical or psychological treatment.

The author and publisher are in no way liable for any misuse of the material. The author nor any facilitators accept responsibility or liability for any outcomes, reactions, or consequences resulting from a child's participation in the Targeted EFT process. By providing consent, parents, guardians, or caregivers acknowledge their responsibility for the child's wellbeing and are encouraged to consult a qualified healthcare professional if they have any concerns before, during, or after using this technique.

DEDICATION

**"When we are no longer able to change a situation,
we are challenged to change ourselves."**

— **Victor Frankl**

To all the children, teenagers, and adults who are struggling to make sense of and cope with the issues and challenges they have experienced in their life—and who continue to do their best, seeking effective help where they can.

To the parents, teachers, and adults who have been there—and now care enough to help the children and teenagers in need to feel safer and cope better within themselves.

To those people who care, I say "onwards and upwards".

"It is easier to build up a child, than it is to repair an adult. Adults and parents, need to choose their words and actions wisely around children."

— **Adapted from an unknown source**

CONTENTS

ABOUT THIS BOOK, EXPECTATIONS, AND IMPORTANT NOTICES vii

    Realistic Expectations vii

    Safeguarding and Duty of Care vii

    If You Feel Triggered or Distressed viii

PREFACE x

INTRODUCTION 1

    How to Use This Book 1

    Who This Book Is For 2

    Important Notes on Safety and Care 3

    My Hope for This Book 3

PART ONE 5

CHAPTER 1: HOW CHILDREN ARE SHAPED BY THEIR PARENTS AND HOME ENVIRONMENT 7

    Foundations for Life: Personal Care for Health, Confidence, Self-Esteem, and Self-Worth 8

    Health Suggestion: Read Product Ingredient Labels 9

    Understanding Their Bodies and Developing Self-Awareness 9

    Girls and Their Menstrual Cycles 10

    The Precious Gift of Sexual Education 12

    Being a Positive Role Model for Children 16

    The Importance of Creating a Safe Home 17

    Boundaries Within the Family and Home 18

Feelings a Child May Experience Based on the Topics Shared in This Chapter 21

Summary 22

CHAPTER 2: CHILDREN IN THE FAMILY 23

The Pressure of Being a Parent 23

Ways Children Survive and Cope With Their Parents and Family 24

The Conscious Survival-Focused Mind in Children and Adults 25

The Need for Children to Experience Effective Therapy Such as Targeted EFT 26

Children's Survival Strategies: Role-playing 28

Feelings a Child May Experience Based on the Topics Shared in This Chapter 37

Summary 38

CHAPTER 3: THE IMPACT OF CHANGING FAMILY DYNAMICS 39

Parental Stress Impacts the Family and Home Dynamic 39

The Challenge for Children With Separation and Divorce 40

The Stress of Domestic War Zones 41

Life Goes on: Healthy Parenting and Co-Parenting 44

The Learning Curves of Life 46

Extreme Separation Situations 48

Feelings a Child May Experience Based on the Topics Shared in This Chapter 49

Summary 50

CHAPTER 4: CHILD BULLYING, EXPLOITATION, AND ONLINE SAFETY 51

Bullying and Its Origins 52

Challenges With Social Interaction for Children at School 52

Understanding Bullying by Children 54

Cyberbullying: A Growing Problem 55

Protecting Kids Online: The Need for Regular Parental Supervision 57

Fear, Intimidation, Bullying, Depression and Overwhelm: The Factors Contributing to Suicide 61

Other Schooling Options, Including Home Schooling 63

Adolescence on Netflix 2025: A Wake-Up Call for Parents 65

Feelings a Child May Experience Based on the Topics Shared in This Chapter 70

Summary 71

CHAPTER 5: SEXUAL ABUSE AND VIOLATION TRAUMA 73

Defining Sexual Abuse and Violation Trauma 74

The Impact of Pornography on School-Aged Children 75

Impacts of Sexual Abuse and Violation on a Child or Teenager 77

Feelings a Child May Experience Based on the Topics Shared in This Chapter 80

Summary 81

CONCLUSION 82

Moving Forward with Care and Confidence 82

PART TWO: THE WORKBOOK 83

CHAPTER 6: FACILITATOR'S ROLE AND RESPONSIBILITIES 85

Who Can Be a Facilitator? 85

What is the Facilitator's Role? 86

Why Parental Consent is Important 87

CHAPTER 7: PREPARING A CHILD FOR TARGETED EFT 89

Identifying a Child Who Can Benefit from Targeted EFT 90

CHAPTER 8: TARGETED EFT TAPPING STATEMENTS FOR CHILDREN 95

Tapping Statements by Category with Explanations 97

Parents, Siblings, and Family (PSF) 97

Upset and Angry (UA) 100

Rejection and Abandonment (RA) 102

Bullying and Conflict (BC) 104

Bullying and Racism (BR) 107

Bullying LGBTQIA+ (BL) 110

Bullying and Disability (BD) 112

Bullying Actions (BA) 115

Abuse and Violation (AV) 117

Overwhelm and Depression (OD) 121

Completion Statements (CS) 123

Modifying Tapping Statements 126

Example of Choosing Tapping Statements for a Child Experiencing Stress . 128

CHAPTER 9: LEARNING TO FACILITATE AND PRACTICE THE TARGETED EFT PROCESS 133

Watch the Tutorial Videos 133

What May Happen When Facilitating a Tapping Session with a Child 135

What to Expect at the Conclusion of a Tapping Session with a Child 136

Targeted EFT Is Scalable 137

CHAPTER 10: PREPARING FOR AND FACILITATING TARGETED EFT SESSIONS 139

    PART 1A: HOME-BASED TAPPING 139

    PART 1B: SCHOOL-BASED TAPPING 141

    PART 2: GATHERING INFORMATION AND SELECTING THE TAPPING STATEMENTS 142

    PART 3: THE TARGETED EFT TAPPING SEQUENCE 145

    PART 4: CONCLUDING THE TAPPING SESSION 152

FREQUENTLY ASKED QUESTIONS 153

RESOURCES 157

    Essential Documents for a Tapping Session with a Child 157

    Tapping Video Links 158

    Further Reading 158

REPORTING CONCERNS: ABUSE, BULLYING, OR CYBERBULLYING 159

ACKNOWLEDGMENTS 161

ABOUT THE AUTHOR 163

CONTACT US 167

ABOUT THIS BOOK, EXPECTATIONS, AND IMPORTANT NOTICES

This book presents the insights and experiences of the author, Paul Boulton. It shares the knowledge, perspectives, and wisdom gained from more than 20 years of working as a therapist and conducting thousands of sessions with clients, using the specialized version of Tapping he developed, known as Targeted Energy Focused Tapping (Targeted EFT).

This book provides readers with a tool that, when used with children, can help reduce their stress, anxiety, tension, overthinking, and more, while supporting greater clarity, self-love, self-awareness, and wellbeing.

Realistic Expectations

While Paul Boulton believes that the Targeted EFT process can be beneficial for most people, he makes no claims to suggest that all children, teenagers, or adults will benefit. In his opinion, there is no single process that can help everyone. However, those with the need, intention, and capacity to engage with the process presented here may experience meaningful benefits.

Safeguarding and Duty of Care

While many children may benefit from this Tapping process, it is not intended to replace medical or psychological treatment.

Some children with learning difficulties or mental health issues may find it challenging to follow the Tapping process. If you are unsure whether this process is suitable for your child, it is recommended to consult with their doctor before engaging the child in a Tapping session.

Also, if a child discloses or suggests that they have experienced abuse, neglect, deprivation, domestic instability, or violence, appropriate action must be taken. In most countries, school staff are legally required to report suspected abuse to child protection services or the police.

Facilitators working in home settings also have a duty to report any suspected abuse. Authorities are trained to handle these situations with care, prioritizing the child's safety. Please check the specific reporting requirements for your region, as laws vary by state and country.

If You Feel Triggered or Distressed

If you find yourself feeling triggered or stressed by any of the content presented in this book, please consider using my Detachment Statement provided below. This tool is featured in my eBook, *Do Detachment Daily*, but I am sharing a specifically worded version here for those who may need it.

Start by taking a deep breath in and out through your nose, then read the following either aloud, quietly to yourself, or in your mind:

> *"I fully and freely forgive and release my mind, and all the people, hurts, and challenges of my life, and let them go to their own and best happiness; and my mind, and all the people, hurts, and challenges of my life, fully and freely forgive and release me, and let me go to my own and best happiness."*

Repeat this five to ten times, or as often as needed, until you feel calm.

About the Book

You can use this Detachment Statement any time you feel stressed, anxious, worried, or overwhelmed. For example, you might say it five times in the morning, again at midday, and once more in the evening before bed—continuing until you feel calm.

PREFACE

In my therapy work over the years, I have found that many of the challenges and issues my adult clients struggle with originated in their childhood—often linked to the circumstances that impacted their parents and family. The old saying, *"the apple doesn't fall far from the tree,"* comes to mind.

In my view, this means we tend to unconsciously adopt our parents' fears and ways of thinking, reacting, and being. As with the stories of my clients—and myself, for a time—these unstable and fearful situations often lead to communication fears and issues and an inability to speak up for one's wishes and needs, or even to know what they are, could be, or should be.

Over time, these confusing mental beliefs and pressures created an identity crisis of sorts for me, fueled by low self-love and self-worth. This led me to sometimes making difficult and clunky interpersonal, work, and life choices—that only increased the stress, anxiety, rejection, abandonment, and confusion I was already overwhelmed by.

All of these seemingly negative fears, beliefs, and experiences set me on a path of self-discovery, driven by a desire to understand why I thought and felt the way I did. I was in my 20s at the time, and over the next decade, I attended many personal development and healing workshops. These workshops often came with physical or mental challenges. One included a static line parachute jump from 2,000 feet; other workshops included fire walks across 1,100-degree coals (I have done four so far), to contemplate my ability to test my own mind-over-matter fears and beliefs.

Preface

This personal journey helped me to understand that the most important thing I could do—once I had found my way and rediscovered myself—would be to help and inspire other people who felt lost, used up, or abused to reconnect with their heart, passion, and soul so they could begin to live a new life in a more self-loving and creative way.

In the early 2000s, I was working as a professional psychic, offering readings and guidance. Around that time, I read the EFT Manual[1] and learned about Emotional Freedom Techniques. Soon after, I began evolving the method to work more effectively for my client's needs—and that is when Targeted Energy Focused Tapping (Targeted EFT) was born. I have been using it ever since to support children, teenagers and adults alike.

The combination of my personal experiences and my work as a therapist has inspired me to write this book. *Helping Kids Rise and Shine* offers readers a foundation on which to build their own new levels of understanding, awareness, compassion, kindness, and growth—while also helping scared, lost children along the way.

—**Paul Boulton**

---

[1] Craig, G. (2003) *Newcomer message from Gary Craig*. [eNewsletter]. The Gary Craig Official EFT™ Training Centres.

INTRODUCTION

How to Use This Book

Part One of this book, *Helping Kids Rise and Shine*, provides the reader with an overview of the challenges and opportunities that many children face from childhood through to their early teens—a time of intense physical, mental, emotional, and social growth.

I share insights and perspectives on how, I believe, many children are attempting to manage their feelings, make decisions, and navigate their lives within challenging family dynamics and other negative influences. All of these factors affect how a child sees and feels about themselves, and how well they respond to and interact with others.

Part Two: The Workbook provides a scaled-down version of the Targeted EFT process I use with my clients in my therapy practice. Using the step-by-step guidelines provided, the reader can become the facilitator, equipped to guide a child or teenager through the Targeted EFT process.

In my view, once a child's mind is in shock, it remains in shock. This poses a challenge for most forms of therapy, as they need to access the depths of the mind to uncover where the conscious survival-focused mind has buried the memories from the shock and traumatic issues it has experienced.

The Targeted EFT process 'unlocks the shock' and 'unlocks the block' that the conscious survival-focused mind created to seal off these challenging, stressful topics, and issues. The process helps the child by reducing the amount of fear, stress, shock, trauma, and overwhelm—whether current or past—by accessing the painful and traumatic memories stored by their mind. By the end of the 30-minute process, the child can often feel calmer and clearer within themselves, ready to move on with their life in exciting new ways.

One of the many benefits this book offers to parents and caring adults is that the Targeted EFT process can be used to support a child or teenager as soon as possible after the fright, shock, abuse, or trauma they have experienced.

By doing so, we may be able to help prevent the child's conscious survival-focused mind from creating and resorting to coping strategies to mask their hurt and overwhelm. This is particularly important in situations where parents do not have access to, or cannot afford to see the doctors, child psychologists, or other professionals who might assist their child.

Who This Book Is For

This book is designed for parents, teachers, and caring adults who want to learn to facilitate this Tapping process to help support children recover from the stressful experiences they have been exposed to that has left them feeling sad, scared, nervous, confused, depressed or traumatized.

It empowers the adults who learn how to facilitate the Targeted EFT process to work with children and help them to transform their issues and negative feelings and boost their self-love, awareness, courage and determination.

Whether you are new to Tapping or have some experience, this book offers clear guidance and practical step-by-step instructions to facilitate the Targeted EFT process, both at home or at school.

Introduction

Important Notes on Safety and Care

While Targeted EFT offers many benefits, it is important to understand it is not a replacement for medical or psychological care. Readers are encouraged to consult healthcare professionals when needed. This book aims to empower adults to support children with compassion and safe practices.

My Hope for This Book

My hope is that this book becomes a valuable and widely used educational and therapy-based resource, to help children **rise and shine** as they face the challenges and opportunities that life presents them. Which, one day, may lead to these same children learning the Targeted EFT Tapping process so they too can help other children in need to **rise and shine**.

PART ONE

1

HOW CHILDREN ARE SHAPED BY THEIR PARENTS AND HOME ENVIRONMENT

"The family is the first school for young children, and parents are powerful models."
— **John Bradshaw,**
Homecoming: Reclaiming and Championing Your Inner Child

From birth to five years of age, babies, and children undergo an enormous range of changes and skill-building. They not only face the demands of crawling, walking, and navigating in their physical environment but also must learn speech, language, gestures, and communication.

All of these challenges are necessary to enhance their chances of surviving within their family and eventually prepare them for life beyond their home.

During their early years children are open and curious about their life. With few filters or boundaries in place, they express how they feel, say what they want, and when they want it. From their perspective, they are the center of their known Universe.

At this time, children are at their most physically, mentally, and emotionally vulnerable and dependent. They are especially sensitive to the moods, feelings, words, agendas, issues, addictions, and expressions used in the home, particularly from their parents and siblings. We have all lived through this experience.

To survive, children's minds must stay vigilant and adapt to the challenges and possible threats around them. They must quickly assess all situations they experience and judge them as good, bad, safe, unsafe, etc.

Over time, children will acquire perspectives, thoughts, beliefs, and fears about people, places, and the world they live in and experience. This can include making sense of their parents' and siblings', opinions, beliefs, fears, and experiences.

As children grow and develop their personalities, their egos become a strong part of who they are becoming, their preferences, and their ability to interact with others and defend themselves. As they become an independent person, this brings with it the aspects of self-determination, willpower, preferences, opinions, identity, etc.

For the parents, the arrival of their child's ego will be evident as soon as the child says 'no'. From that point on, their child's will and determination will be another factor for the parents to love, manage, and negotiate with.

Foundations for Life: Personal Care for Health, Confidence, Self-Esteem, and Self-Worth

Usually by the age of five, children have become more independent and are able to demonstrate to their parents that they can properly wash, clean, and dress themselves, including brushing their hair and teeth.

Providing children with clean clothing and underwear daily is also important, as this positively contributes to them feeling clean and confident, which boosts their self-image, self-worth, and self-esteem when interacting and playing with other children.

I know this sounds obvious enough, doesn't it? While this may be a normal situation for your family, it is not the case for all families, and those children have to face the consequences, challenges, negative comments, and potential threats of alienation that come with it.

Parents may hope that once shown, their children will naturally prioritize their self-care, washing and bathing requirements daily, but it is important not to make that assumption. Take the time to check in with your children, ask them directly if they have taken a shower, washed their hair, etc.

As children grow and reach puberty, many boys may decide that they don't feel like changing their clothes, bathing or brushing their teeth on a daily basis anymore. For boys who make these 'stinky' decisions, it can become more difficult to manage in a single-parent home, especially for the mother, as the boy may ignore her requests.

Health Suggestion: Read Product Ingredient Labels

It is becoming increasingly important for aware parents to ensure the soaps, shampoos, and conditioners they provide for themselves, and their children do not contain harsh or harmful ingredients. Pure, old-fashioned soap may be a safer option than highly fragrant body washes, which can cause skin irritations and other issues. Take the time to read the ingredient labels and research what they are online. Good, safe products are often priced similarly to fancy, toxic chemical-laden products.

Understanding Their Bodies and Developing Self-Awareness

As boys and girls grow, they naturally become interested in their own bodies, how they work and function, and many will quickly learn what is or is not socially acceptable behavior in public.

For children, their self-awareness, self-image, self-worth, and self-esteem is also developing. Not necessarily their fashion sense, or ability to gauge the best time to wear their favorite outfit, or to comply when specific shoes, clothing, uniforms, etc., are required.

Children are influenced by the opinions, comments, and reactions they receive from their family, friends, peers, and others. For the most part, children will want to be accepted, included, and fit in with the 'group'. When this doesn't happen, they can begin to feel isolated, rejected, inferior, teased, or unworthy, which can lead to them feeling sad, upset, and depressed.

Children are impressionable and susceptible to comparing themselves negatively to others, often believing the negative comments they hear from those they interact with. These experiences can significantly influence their view of themselves in a negative way.

Girls and Their Menstrual Cycles

Sensitive and informative discussions are needed with girls at the right time before they reach puberty. These conversations are very important for supporting and guiding them in how to best manage their emotions, hormonal changes, early sexualized feelings, menstrual cycles, and self-care.

This includes helping them understand that it is a natural bodily process that prepares them for the possibility of pregnancy. I know this is not what parents want for the 12-year-old, but it is important they understand how unplanned pregnancies can occur.

Girls will benefit from understanding what to expect during the stages of their menstrual cycle including mood changes that come with pre-menstrual syndrome (PMS), as well as the physical discomfort and pain they may experience. They should also be informed about remedies and products that may help.[2] [3] There are many helpful websites available to help parents with these discussions.

Providing the knowledge and the appropriate products to use before their menstrual cycle begins can be incredibly helpful for a blossoming young girl. While this is a natural part of their development, it would be beneficial if parents could offer loving support during this time.

Single fathers may find it helpful to call upon a trusted woman to assist in guiding and sharing with their daughters. Additionally, male siblings in the family should be advised about the important changes their sister is going through and the need for them to be sensitive, respectful, and gentle with her, and other girls and women they interact with.

As a therapist, it has been alarming to hear how many of my female clients, when they were young girls, were not properly informed by their mothers or parents about how to manage their menstrual cycles, which led to them feeling much shame and embarrassment.

Puberty can bring unwanted physical changes and attention, which can be particularly confronting for both girls and boys as they adjust to their developing adult bodies. From growth spurts and changes in shape to acne and weight gain, these changes can create a lot of pressure on a child's mental and emotional ability to cope.

Most parents would hope their children will grow into being healthy, independent teenagers and adults, preferably with as few cringe-worthy or

---

[2] Raising Children Network. (2024, May 22). *Periods and the menstrual cycle*. https://raisingchildren.net.au/teens/development/periods-hygiene/periods

[3] Anzilotti, A. W. (2024, July). *All about periods*. Nemours Children's Health. https://kidshealth.org/en/teens/menstruation.html

uncomfortable comments and displays as possible. However, this won't happen magically. It requires constant parental vigilance, care, sharing, and support to guide and help your children through all the stages of their lives.

The Precious Gift of Sexual Education

Once the parents have educated their children about self-care, cleanliness, and body awareness, the next important topic is sexual awareness, education, and responsibilities. This may be a gradual process, with age-appropriate information and answers shared over time. The right moment may arise when the children themselves start talking about their classmates having a boyfriend or girlfriend.

Most parents are aware how easy it is to 'gross out' a child or teenager. Just start cuddling in the kitchen, and I'm sure the feedback and opinions that you receive from your children will be swift and harsh, from your teenagers at least.

It is normal for parents to feel a bit awkward and embarrassed about what to say, partly because, back in the day, they were often left to figure it out for themselves. Historically, many parents have dodged and neglected their responsibility and duty of care when it comes to discussing these topics with their children.

It can be beneficial for older children, from aged eight to ten, to learn about the importance of love and sex, what it means to conceive a child, and what they need to know to prevent that from happening.

If parents are reluctant to discuss sexual development, contraception and related topics with their children, they will likely learn about it from their school friends, YouTube or other social media platforms. They may also hear stories and disturbing comments from their siblings, friends, classmates or others, which can add to their confusion and embarrassment.

Parents need to educate, inform, and, at times, sometimes equip their children with the knowledge, resources, and products they may need. It is so important to maintain a healthy level of communication, confidentiality, and privacy with your children during this time, to help them feel informed and supported as they grow into being healthy teenagers.

By doing so, parents remove the topic of sex from the shadows of confusion and shame, bringing it into the light and presenting it as an important aspect of the decisions their children will make as they grow older. This allows parents to impress upon their child family values like waiting for the right partner and time, when they become adults, and both decide to start a family.

Topics such as being in love, choosing a partner, and engaging in sex, and contraception should be revisited when your child becomes a teenager.

How Much Sexual Education Is Too Much?

For many parents, there can be an underlying fear about the possible implications of sharing sexual education information with their children. They may fear that this knowledge could ignite their child's curiosity and passion, leading to concerns and issues later on.

As a therapist, the topics of love, sexual education, and awareness are particularly important to me, as it helps to empower children to wish and dream about their own partners, families, and lives one day. And for teenagers to make better, more informed, and healthier life choices.

I consider it is best to promote the most positive goal to your children that you desire to see. Rather than what usually happens in this scenario where school kids take risks without using contraception, and then unexpectedly find themselves pregnant, leading to major stressful decisions being forced upon them.

Sex education is an important piece of the development puzzle that children need to know about. By providing this information themselves, parents can safely and sensitively present accurate information over time to help and guide their children to become aware, mature, responsible, knowledgeable, functional teenagers, and eventually adults.

Denial of Parental Responsibility

Parents that say they are too busy, disinterested, in denial, or are afraid to talk about sexual education with their children, are ultimately putting them at risk by leaving them undereducated and unprepared for the next stages of their lives.

While children can physically mature quickly, developing adult-like bodies, their mental and emotional growth progresses more slowly. Teaching children about love, partnership, sexual education, and how to establish and maintain healthy physical boundaries, can benefit them in many ways.

This education can help children understand and know the difference between appropriate and inappropriate touch, as well as acceptable behavior when interacting with others.

This important information and awareness will help children build their own solid foundations of body awareness and safety, which can positively influence their self-image, self-worth, self-love, and self-esteem with healthy boundaries.

Both parents play an important role in their children's physical, mental, emotional, psychological, sexual development, as well as in teaching essential skills for life. The attention, care, conversations, openness to discuss topics, and support that parents provide their children can help them enormously. Even if the parent's relationship ends, maintaining and valuing the bond between both parents and their children should remain a priority.

For daughters, the role of the father includes showing her what it means to be safely and respectfully loved by a man, especially as she grows from a girl to a teenager and young woman. It is important for her to live and grow in a safe honoring home, whenever possible, and enjoy a safe, supportive, and accepting relationship with both her mother and father.

This can help her to develop her self-confidence and a strong sense of self, enabling her to establish and enforce healthy boundaries, as well as an awareness of her legal right for consent. This means that she has the legal right to determine who she will allow to engage in any degree of intimate touch and or sex with her. She will need this knowledge to help her navigate interactions with boys, men, and other adults who may attempt to tease, bully, control, and manipulate her throughout her life.

Sons need a healthy, responsive, father figure to be with, to share stories with, and to learn from about the importance of respectful communication with their mother, sisters, and females in their lives, including friends, schoolteachers, classmates, and others they interact with.

The importance of this is that, if these examples do not come from their father or another prominent male in their life, the boy may learn from his peer group instead. Often these groups can be harsh, inappropriate, rude, disrespectful, and promote sexual objectification, exploitive interactions with girls, bullying, violence, and manipulative behavior, which may even attract the attention of the police.

Single mothers may need to play both parental roles in a family, but they cannot truly replace a safe man. In times like these, safe male friends can be important for talking, interacting, and being accessible to the children, both boys and girls.

Pronouns and Sexuality Choices

The 2020s are very different from times past, with children and teenagers now able to more openly explore and make decisions about their personal preferences, gender, sexuality, pronouns, and life choices.

The best way for parents to support their child at such times is to be open to talking to them about these topics when the child brings them up. It is important for parents not to freak out, and to suspend their judgments and personal views during these discussions. The thoughts your child expresses may simply be random thoughts and questions.

Expressions of anger and hostility at this time could lead to your child excluding you from their future conversations about this and other topics.

Being a Positive Role Model for Children

Parents are usually the first role models' children are exposed to. At its most basic, a parent is a person or a couple who have either produced or decided to commit to raising a child or children.

In the best situations, parental role modeling includes the ability to positively influence, nurture, guide, love, support, and direct the mental, emotional, physical, and spiritual health and development of the child or children they raise. It is a natural survival trait of children to trust and be open to acts of kindness, acceptance, and inclusion, that their parents or family provide.

The way parents speak, care, share, and display love, have fun, manage themselves, along with their finances and stressful situations, affect the mental, emotional, spiritual, psychological, and physical health, safety, stability, and confidence of the children they raise and influence.

As children grow, they may encounter and accept new role models who have the time to listen, talk with, accept, and support them. These role models could be the parents of their friends, an aunt, a safe neighbor, a teacher's aide, a shopkeeper who looks out for them, or someone who becomes a friend. For some children, these people may become their 'family of choice', with whom they share parts of their lives.

A positive role model for children is someone who is safe, friendly, respectful, and appropriate in both public and private interactions with children. They communicate respectfully, dedicate time to the child, believe in them, and inspire them.

While both parents will love their children, the way each parent expresses that love and care can vary. For example, one parent may show affection by providing material support, such as sending the children to the best schools, giving gifts, or providing holidays. This parent may have a more analytical nature and may not be as physically affectionate. The other parent may prefer to express love through physical affection, nurturing, cooking for the children, and actively supporting their interests, hobbies, and after-school activities.

It is beneficial for children to appreciate the different ways their parents, grandparents, relatives, and other people they encounter show them love. They can learn how to share in supportive ways, be kind, and understand that there are various ways to define a family, relatives, and friendships.

The Importance of Creating a Safe Home

In my opinion, our home should be considered a sacred space—a special place where we live with our partner, children, pets, and more. It holds our most important possessions and is where we share, play, rest, relax, communicate, and spend quality time together. Our home also reflects the values and qualities that are important to us, including love, nurturing, respect, appreciation, and healthy boundaries.

As parents—or as a single parent—we set the tone, mood, intent, language, energy, and activities that swirl and flow through the family home. Family members, relatives, friends, and others who respect these values and contribute to this positive atmosphere may be welcomed and invited to join us in our space.

It is important for children to feel safe in their home, to have a sense of belonging, and believe in the values their family lives by. This can best be achieved when there is a genuine, inclusive connection among the family members living in the home. In a perfect world, the family members would express love, care, and respect for one another sincerely and consistently. These positive examples help children learn, experience, and value the importance of a safe, caring, and loving home.

It is okay to dream for this, isn't it? I saw a quote today *"Become the adult you needed as a child."*

Boundaries Within the Family and Home

Learning about love, respect, rules, and the consequences of actions is an important and natural part of child's development in the family and home. When a child lacks an understanding of sharing, caring, respect, and healthy communication with their parents, siblings, and others, it can quickly create challenges in their life.

In my opinion, it is the responsibility of parents to teach their children the basic principles of right and wrong actions and behavior. This includes appropriate ways of speaking to and interacting with others, as well as respecting other people's possessions in all situations.

Additionally, encouraging children to apologize when they have done wrong can greatly support their maturity and their moral, mental, social, and emotional development. This skill becomes much easier for children to adopt when they see their parents modeling it by speaking up, apologizing, and acknowledging mistakes or differences of opinion within their own relationships, home, and elsewhere.

Advantages of Setting Healthy Standards and Boundaries at Home

Parents who share loving and stable values, communicate openly and honestly, and occasionally disagree but resolve conflicts fairly and respectfully, provide a healthy foundation for their children to follow.

Parents who offer words of support and encouragement, use appropriate language in the home, give balanced and constructive feedback, and demonstrate the ability to apologize when needed, serve as great role models for their children. Their actions contribute to their children's mental, emotional, and social development, preparing them for school, relationships, and life in society.

How to Help Empower Children with Creating Personal Boundaries

Things parents can do to help support and empower their children in creating and maintaining healthy personal boundaries include:

1. Encourage their children to talk about their day, helping them become familiar with speaking up and expressing how they feel, while knowing that their parents are listening and genuinely care. Open communication builds trust and will enable children to feel comfortable and safe sharing their concerns, challenges, and experiences.

2. Encourage their children to be alert and trust their feelings, senses, and awareness when a person's mood, energy, words, or actions change in a way that makes the child feel unsafe or threatened by them.

3. Teach their children how to speak up and seek help from an adult if they feel nervous, vulnerable, uncomfortable or sense danger.

4. Teach their children that it is okay to say "no" to an adult or an unknown person, and to move away to a safe person or place when they feel uncomfortable or scared. Instruct them on how to call out loudly or scream for help if necessary to attract attention and help from others.

5. Empower their children to ignore and resist unwanted comments or actions. Explain what unwanted suggestions, comments, or actions look, sound and feel like. Do not assume they will automatically recognize them.

6. Explain to their children the importance of not keeping secrets from them or trusted adults, emphasizing that they should always feel safe sharing anything that makes them uncomfortable or worried.

7. Provide age-appropriate education about personal safety, body anatomy, and personal boundaries to children. If parents need resources to assist them, check online as there are many books and websites available to help both parents and children learn about these topics. In the US, some schools are now mandated by the *Erin's Law*[4] legislation to teach about personal body safety, boundaries, and recognizing and responding to abusive

---

[4] Erin's Law. (n.d.). *Erin's Law: Mandating child sexual abuse prevention education in schools.* https://www.erinslaw.org/

situations. BASE's Erin's Law curriculum[5] meets all requirements mandated by the legislation.

By equipping children with the confidence to recognize and speak up about their thoughts, fears, issues, concerns, and physical boundaries early on, we can enhance their awareness, courage, and ability to navigate challenges as they grow into their teenage years and beyond. This is important because predatory types know how to stress and intimidate children into being quiet and compliant.

If children have a mobile phone, parents can arrange to have the contact information of a few trusted friends, relatives, their school admin office, and the police added to their children's phone address book. Also, parents can install a location tracking app on the child's mobile phone.[6][7] Always ensure that this feature remains active, as it may provide critical information to help locate your child quickly in an emergency.

Feelings a Child May Experience Based on the Topics Shared in This Chapter

The negative feelings that babies and children may experience include:

Sadness, Nervousness, Anxiety, Fear, Fright, Confusion, Shock, Rejection, and Abandonment.

---

[5] 7 Mindsets. (2024). *New in 2024! Erin's Law curriculum series* https://7mindsets.com/base/new-in-2024-erins-law-curriculum-series/

[6] Findmykids. (n.d.). *Real-time location tracking.* https://findmykids.org/features/real-time-location

[7] KidSafe Seal. (n.d.). *Certified products* https://www.kidsafeseal.com/certifiedproducts.html

Summary

1. Children from birth to age five are highly vulnerable and sensitive to their home environment, and need to learn speech, movement, and communication skills.

2. To survive the children are naturally vigilant and must adapt to their family and home, assessing situations as safe or unsafe.

3. As children grow, they develop self-awareness about their bodies, and their need for cleanliness and self-care.

4. As children approach the ages of 10 and 11, conversations about puberty, menstrual cycles, physical and emotional changes help guide them through these transitions.

5. Sexual education and discussions on consent and respect are essential for children's development and understanding of healthy relationships.

6. Parents need to be good role models and create a safe, supportive home environment with clear boundaries to foster emotional security and positive behavior in their children.

2

CHILDREN IN THE FAMILY

"The family is the primary place of woundedness and healing. It is where our scripts are written and where they can be rewritten."
— John Bradshaw,
Homecoming: Reclaiming and Championing Your Inner Child

The Pressure of Being a Parent

When people partner, they bring with them their hopes, dreams, wishes, and the experiences of their life journey to date, including their own unaddressed issues and dysfunctional behaviors into the new relationship. This can, at times, create friction and challenges for both partners to manage and deal with.

Once the couple becomes parents, these unresolved issues can continue, making it difficult for both partners and their children to cope and live with. While most parents would like to handle and manage the stress they are exposed to in a positive, balanced way, no one can remain calm and balanced all the time.

Children learn from watching their parents react and respond to the good times and the challenging times they experience. Sometimes, the parents will handle situations well and achieve successful outcomes. Other times, due to the internal and external pressures of life, relationship demands, financial pressures, and the choices they make, their plans may fail, and everyone in the family has to live with the consequences.

Occasionally, life's challenges can be overwhelming when a parent loses a job, gets injured, develops an illness, becomes depressed, gets arrested, leaves the family, dies etc.

When life changes dramatically, situations must be reassessed to fit the new reality. This is the process of 'adulting', and during these times, the children will watch, hear, feel, think, and adjust themselves according to the choices and reactions their parents, family, or guardians make.

During those times, the parents may not have always been at their most aware, kind, loving, honest, balanced, or effective in how they communicated and interacted within the relationship and family dynamic.

It is true for most parents that they did the best they could at the time, to the level of stress, awareness, composure, honesty, and integrity that they could manage.

Ways Children Survive and Cope with Their Parents and Family

As children grow, their conscious mind naturally acquires a range of coping mechanisms in their attempt to manage the stress, pressures and idiosyncrasies of their parents, siblings, and home environment. Children also come to see their parents' words, expressions, habits, and behaviors as 'normal' ways for them to speak and behave.

Parental fears, issues, and beliefs can manifest in the home as habits, rules, and expectations for the children to live by, and these may change without notice, leaving the children to sometimes feel confused, stressed, and overwhelmed.

Children can easily sense tension in the home, and during these times, they can feel scared, nervous, uncertain, and unsafe. These tensions may contribute to children developing stress responses, coping behaviors, eating issues, attention or speech issues, sleeping problems, and so on.

For survival reasons, a child's conscious mind observes, reacts to, and memorizes the moods of their parents, siblings, and others they interact with. As the child grows and attempts to interact with people they encounter, they will often mimic the expressions, mannerisms and responses they have heard, observed, remembered and experienced to date, for better or worse.

It is in these early developmental years that a child becomes familiar with the aspects of their own mind that shape the perspectives they use to interpret, see, and react to the world around them.

The Conscious Survival-Focused Mind in Children and Adults

An easy way to understand the mind is to consider it as having two parts: the subconscious mind or greater mind, which knows all things and is connected to every aspect of your destiny path and the greater good.

Then there is the conscious mind, which has the role of guiding you in managing the choices, opportunities, experiences, and challenges that occur in your life, with the hope and goal of helping you prosper and thrive.

The survival-focused mind is a subset of the conscious mind —what I refer to as the conscious survival-focused mind. In childhood, its role is to notice and react to potential threats—real or perceived—and to issues it considers a challenge or danger to the child. It then attempts to respond by defending, protecting, and steering the child away from them.

The goal of the conscious survival-focused mind is to keep the child safe. When it deems it necessary, it generates doubts and fears, which can restrict and limit their willingness to take risks, trust themselves, and follow through with their desires.

The consequences of these negative perspectives for the child may include feelings of nervousness, anxiety, and a lack of self-trust or confidence. This can affect their ability to learn how to ride a bike or a pony, climb trees or in playgrounds, dance, sing, express themselves in public, swim properly, or participate in team sports like football, basketball, baseball etc.

There may be many times when a child will wonder whether their conscious survival-focused mind is truly on their side, working for their greater good and best outcomes.

We know that the conscious survival-focused mind is totally committed to the survival of the child, at least in theory. In practice, however, one might consider it too cautious, too controlling, and too conservative in how it perceives the world and the challenges that it identifies out there.

In reality, it often just needs a 'spring clean' and new guidelines to reset its ability to identify genuine threats in an ever-changing world, without getting stuck in a hypervigilant, defensive state, that makes the child more prone to alarm, exhaustion, and overwhelm.

The Need for Children to Experience Effective Therapy Such as Targeted EFT

When a child feels unloved, ignored, isolated, lonely, rejected, or abandoned by their parents or siblings, the confusion and stress they experience can be overwhelming. Often, they will have no way to deal with these feelings.

So, their mind stores these challenging issues deep within the conscious survival focused mind, keeping the child in a state of being vigilant in an attempt to manage or ward off the next threat they encounter. Over time, these unresolved issues accumulate, and the childhood feelings of being unloved, ignored, unworthy, isolated, lonely, or depressed carry over and expand into their teenage years.

This happens for two reasons. First, their mind has not changed its decision to store all uncomfortable issues and experiences deep within its internal mental library. Second, most people in society are never taught how to effectively process the hurts, fears, and unresolved issues carried over from childhood and their teenage years.

These types of issues and challenges are often considered normal parts of childhood and teenage years, with the belief that we will eventually learn to live with them. For those who struggle to cope with their issues, there are medical services available, and doctors who can refer them to the appropriate support.

For those people who want to be more involved in their own healing-based journey, there are various therapy-based processes available that they can explore and experience.

In my view, these unresolved challenging issues stored within the person's mind will continue to grow, fester, and manifest themselves in unhealthy ways throughout a person's life. These negative, fear-based thoughts can lead to unhealthy relationships, risky behaviors, poor financial decisions, and addictive behaviors—including alcohol, drugs, gambling etc.—all of which can negatively impact both the individual and their family.

This is why effective therapy is needed—to help people process and release these stressful, challenging issues stored deep within their minds.

And also why I wrote this book—to help parents, teachers, and caring adults to learn and facilitate the Targeted EFT process with children in need. This helps the children by reducing the amount of stressful issues their minds have stored, allowing them to see, feel, and respond to their lives in new, healthier ways in the moment.

Children's Survival Strategies: Role-playing

Children have a lot to understand, feel, respond to, integrate, and cope with as they attempt to navigate and survive the family they were born into or live with. This includes figuring out the best ways for them to be, act, and survive while managing the pressures from each of their parents, their parent's relationship, their siblings, and other children within the family home.

Children often engage in survival-based role-playing within the family to help them cope with their parents' mood swings, anger issues, and controlling tendencies. A well-timed action, like a smile, may help keep the child safe and included, but it may not always be effective due to the stress levels and mood of their parent(s).

Some of the types of role-playing included in the list following may come about as a conscious or unconscious reaction to the situation, challenges, and stress the child feels within the family home.

If a particular role proves successful in meeting their needs, the child is likely to continue using it. On the other hand, if the role does not achieve their desired outcomes, they may try different roles.

In these situations, the child's conscious survival-focused mind prioritizes their physical survival, and it is capable of manipulating and influencing many of their actions and choices. In doing so, the child's mind seeks out options that it is willing to pursue and endure to get its needs met. This behavior is driven by the instinctual drive for acceptance, survival, and self-preservation.

Here are some examples of role-playing options a child may engage in depending upon their age, skill level, and needs in a situation:

- The grade-A student.

- The clown.

- The sports star.

- The sickly.

- The whiner.

- The victim.

- The potty-mouth.

- The angry.

- The bully.

- The daredevil/risk-taker.

- The quiet.

- The judgmental.

- The dismissive.

- The supportive.

- The mothering.

- The peacekeeper.

- The helper.

- The martyr.
- The entitled.
- The spoiled.
- The sick.
- The reclusive.
- The loner.
- The dreamer.
- The introvert.
- The angel.
- The devil.
- The animal lover.
- The independent.
- The determined.
- The extrovert.
- The overachiever.
- The attention seeker.
- The controller.
- The starter.
- The finisher.

- The procrastinator.

- The fighter.

- The healer.

- The mediator.

- The suspicious.

- The avoider.

- The cutie/look-at-me.

- The depressed.

- The lifeless.

- The spiritual.

- The cunning.

- The people-pleaser.

- The invisible child who hides.

- The narcissist.

- The intellectual.

- The talker.

- The manipulator.

- The negotiator.

And similar roles, etc. Many of these roles can prove beneficial to the child, and they may become competent at moving between several of them, due to the need and changing circumstances they are facing.

The ability to shift between roles doesn't necessarily end in childhood or teenage years. Some adults may never let go of their childhood role-playing personas, such as 'the people pleaser', 'the martyr', 'the rock star', 'the sports star', or 'the comedian' etc. Or the man with 'the biker' persona, who has the leather jacket, boots, and t-shirt, but doesn't own a motorbike.

Which of the roles do you recognize in your own children or in yourself, either now or when you were a child?

In the last decade, we have become familiar with the rise of 'the influencer' role. This role can lead a person to expand and adapt their self-created personas to meet the pressures they face, attempting to craft and project an image of themselves that aligns with the glitz and glamour of their hoped-for celebrity status.

Self-Protection and the Reactions of a Child's Conscious Survival-Focused Mind

From an early age, a child's mind begins to create categories encompassing their thoughts, tastes, preferences, as well as feelings, responses, and reactions. This information is stored in the subconscious mind, ready to be launched at a moment's notice if the situation changes, whether it becomes joyful and exciting, or threatening. Depending on the child's expectations and mood in the moment, they could react well or badly.

For example, as a child's birthday approaches, their family and relatives may tell them how exciting it is that they will soon be a year older, and that they have presents for them. Hearing this, the child becomes excited, knowing they are getting presents, there will be a cake, and there might even be a party for them to enjoy and be celebrated. As a result, their expectations and excitement build towards the big day. However, when the birthday plans don't go as expected due to a family disruption, the child becomes stressed, tense, angry, confused, and overwhelmed.

When a child feels scared and shocked by a stressful and intense situation, their mind will often trigger a survival reaction, the 'fight, flight, or freeze' response.

Depending upon the size of the challenge or threat, and the degree of overwhelm the threat presents, the child's conscious survival-focused mind will determine how to survive the threat and react to the situation.

Possible responses can include:

- Fighting.

- Running away.

- Ignoring the threat.

- Crying.

- Calling or screaming for help.

- Freezing and keeping still, being immobilized.

- Dissociating.

- Attempting to numb down the feelings and responses.

- Stashing the topic away.

- Attempting to deny its existence, or that it happened.

- Using sugar or sweets to help them cope with the pressures.

To the conscious survival-focused mind, it doesn't actually want to see or deal with these issues ever again, mainly because the topic has already scared or traumatized the child. Their mind has no desire to reopen that can of worms.

The freeze response is particularly difficult for a child's mind to manage, as the conscious mind has to generate from within itself enough energy to override the fight/flight response and create the immobilizing, freeze response.

The freeze response is triggered when a child feels so scared, anxious, and overwhelmed due to the fears, uncertainty, abuse, and violation that they have experienced or are currently enduring. They may believe they cannot be saved, or rescued, and fear that the abuse will never end. As a result, the mind may feel they have no other option but to dissociate in order to help the child survive the fearful, abusive situation they are experiencing.

To be clear, the fight, flight, and freeze response has its place in the moment, when a child or person's mind perceives and is confronted with a serious threat.

An Example of Challenging Childhood Experiences

If we use a child-based issue as an example, let us consider the first time a child performed, sang or danced in public.

Imagine this child is feeling excited. They have practiced for weeks and feel encouraged and supported by their parents, who loved hearing and watching them practice.

On the day of the performance, the child is all excited, dressed in their special clothes, and ready to go.

But when it is time for the actual performance, things do not go according to their expectations or plan. The child becomes a bit shocked and overwhelmed by everyone looking at them, blanks out and can't sing, forgets the words, becomes stressed, nervous, and cries.

Yes, an uncomfortable experience for them, for sure, and it could have been made worse if someone in the audience had made a comment and everyone laughed.

Due to the shock they experienced, the child's conscious survival-focused mind decided to override and block the child's desire and ability to speak up and express themselves in public in order to avoid feeling scared, afraid, embarrassed, humiliated, laughed at, depressed, or overwhelmed ever again.

To do this it has incepted the thought into the overwhelmed child's memory, *"I am shocked and embarrassed by what has happened, and I will never sing, speak up, or put myself in that sort of situation ever again."*

A few weeks later, the child's parents decide to address the topic in a calm and logical way. They explain to their child that there are different ways to respond to the situation and offer some options for the child to consider. They may say:

1. *"We know you did your best, and we're proud of you. How about taking some lessons to help you feel more prepared next time?"*

2. *"We know how much you love singing. Maybe you would feel more comfortable singing in a choir, where you will have the support of others?"*

The well-intentioned suggestions their parents come up with to help the child may come to no avail, due to the decision the child's conscious survival-focused mind has made to never embarrass themselves, speak up, sing, or be seen in public again.

Decades later, as an adult, they may be called upon to deliver a speech at an important occasion in their life and immediately feel nervous and overwhelmed at the thought of it. They may remember having an issue as a child, but since that was thirty years ago, they may struggle to see the connection.

The problem is that their conscious survival-focused mind has never changed the limiting belief about the fear and embarrassment that singing in public caused them. As a result, that thirty-year-old fear, which remains unaddressed within them, still controls and restricts their ability to express themselves in public. Now, it causes them a new degree of embarrassment, as they find they cannot speak up publicly without feeling dizzy, anxious, overwhelmed and scared.

We can use this same type of example to show how the impact of violation trauma can create overwhelming fears and behavioral changes in a child who was scared, touched, abused, and violated in their childhood. Often, due to the embarrassment and humiliation they experienced, and the fact that they have never spoken up about what happened, or received any help, these issues have remained unaddressed.

This fight, flight, and freeze response can unfortunately lead to decades of stress and fear, making it difficult for the person to speak up, or live and love in healthy ways.

From my perspective as a therapist, helping a child or adult's mind to switch back on by overriding the freeze response may require regular sessions of effective therapy, such as Targeted EFT, as featured in **Part Two: The Workbook**. This is because it is necessary to work through the layers of self-protective mental blocks, beliefs, and barriers that their own conscious survival-focused mind has created and put in place, to bury these issues deep within their subconscious mind.

Children may also benefit from activities to help boost their self-confidence, mental and emotional strength, physical and spatial awareness, objectivity, sensitivity, and responsiveness. These activities can include yoga, tai chi, Qi Gong, dance, martial arts, mindfulness, art-based therapies etc.

Feelings a Child May Experience Based on the Topics Shared in This Chapter

The negative feelings an older child or teenager may experience in the family include:

Fear, Anxiety, Nervousness, Doubt, Insecurity, Helplessness, Hopelessness, Embarrassment, Humiliation, Overwhelm, and Depression.

Summary

1. Parents bring their own unresolved issues into relationships, creating challenges for themselves and their children.

2. The stress parents feel can affect the family dynamic and cause the children to feel unsafe and develop stress responses.

3. Children can cope by adopting survival strategies, such as role-playing different personas.

4. Children need to manage survival-focused reactions, like fight, flight, freeze in response to stress or trauma.

5. Children may benefit from mind-body activities such as dance, yoga, or martial arts to help boost their self-confidence, mental and emotional strength, physical and spatial awareness etc.

3

THE IMPACT OF CHANGING FAMILY DYNAMICS

"The child's primary relationship is with the parent, and if that relationship is disturbed, the child's emotional development is disturbed."
— Gabor Maté,
Hold On to Your Kids: Why Parents Need to Matter More Than Peers

Parental Stress Impacts the Family and Home Dynamic

If you were born to parents who loved each other, communicated well, and had great coping and problem-solving skills, you would have been very lucky indeed. However, most relationships between parents are not anything like this. The stress of managing jobs, finances, their own relationship, and their personal wishes and desires can strain their ability to love each other, communicate effectively, and live happily together.

Good relationships require attentiveness, work, care, love, loyalty, fun, nurturing, honesty, and the contribution of both individuals to maintain a healthy balance.

Instability in family and home environments can create stress and tension for both parents and children. Many factors can affect the relationship between parents, including how they discuss, solve, relate, and handle problems, Issues such as physical and mental health (including depression), work pressures, sex, hormonal issues (such as perimenopause), domestic responsibilities, relationships with relatives, unemployment, financial strain, affairs, alcohol or drug use, gambling, and domestic violence, can all become overwhelming.

These stressors can significantly affect a couple's ability to function well within the home and maintain a healthy marriage. When the love reserves become depleted, this often leads to separation, and ultimately, divorce.

Separation can sometimes involve months of tension and stress before the parents actually begin living apart. During these difficult, sad, and uncertain times, both parents and children will do their best to adapt, cope, and survive the changes within their family dynamic.

It is natural for children to worry, feel sad, and unsettled when their parents separate. The children must first adapt to the absence and stress of one parent no longer living at home. This can lead to feelings of anxiety, sadness, worry, and concern for the parent who has moved out. The children may wonder about how that parent is coping, their wellbeing, where they are living, whether they are eating properly, when they might call, or when they will visit or see them again. They may also worry about whether the parent is feeling lonely, sad or missing them.

The Challenge for Children with Separation and Divorce

Children can be raised in various scenarios, including the traditional two-parent households, single-parent homes, or other situations. Sometimes, grandparents step in and become the primary caregivers, either living within the same home as the parent or commuting to help out regularly.

While separation and divorce are intense and difficult times for everyone involved, they don't have to have a lasting impact on the parents, children, or the broader family unit. Couples who experience separation or divorce have an opportunity to heal, regroup, and create a new way of living. Perhaps even to love again with a new partner if they choose to.

During times of separation and divorce, one of the most important aspects to be mindful of is the mental and emotional well-being of the children. It can be very damaging to a child's development if they are exposed to one parent becoming mean, restrictive, and punishing, financially controlling, verbally abusive, or manipulative toward the other parent.

Despite the hurt and pain each parent may feel, it is important to resist venting or verbally abusing the other parent in the presence of the children. In most cases, the children will still love each parent but may begin to feel that it is no longer safe or easy to talk about their love and feelings for the other parent at home. This can lead to the child feeling they have to stifle and suppress their feelings, which can lead to them creating unhealthy patterns of secrecy and role-playing just to keep the peace in the home.

Separation and divorce are often intense and bitter experiences for the parents, children, and extended family members. Unfortunately, legal battles can sometimes become platforms for financial control, greed, meanness, resentment, and punishment. When this happens, the consequences can extend beyond the ex-partner, creating hardship and unnecessary financial strain that can also impact the wellbeing and stability of the children.

We can only hope that parents choose to approach separation with fairness, effective problem-solving, and a willingness to listen, care, and share responsibilities in ways that support their children. Ideally, they will interact in win/win ways, recognizing that both may need to be present for various important events in their children's lives for years and decades to come.

The Stress of Domestic War Zones

It can be a sad, stressful, and confusing time for both children and parents when the decision to separate and divorce is made. This disruption can sometimes happen quickly, causing instability in the children's routines and home life. Additionally, children may be exposed to the anger, hurt, bitterness, betrayal, and rejection that both their parents may be feeling.

Many divorces and property settlements end up in court and can take years to resolve. In particularly difficult cases, separation can feel like and resemble a war zone of sorts, adding to the emotional strain for everyone involved.

When a relationship ends, the details of the breakup are often not shared with the children in an honest, age-appropriate manner. While relationship breakups happen, it is important to acknowledge that, in most cases, both parents have contributed to it.

For example, one parent—let's say the mother in this case—may aim to depict herself as being 'in the right', blameless, innocent, and the victim, providing only her biased perspectives on what led to the breakup. This manipulative approach may even, at times, extend to implying that the children's actions or behavior contributed to the breakup and their father's departure. *"If only you were better behaved, things would be different."*

With the father absent and unable to share his side of the story, and speak his truth about why the relationship ended, the children are left to speculate. This can sometimes result in the children feeling sad, guilty, confused, and responsible for their parents' breakup.

Unfortunately, during such a difficult time, being honest requires more courage than many people possess. Often, they would rather appear to be 'right' in the moment rather than risk losing their children's acceptance by honestly sharing their part in the breakdown of the relationship.

There may be times when a parent is not told the truth or details about why their partner has left the relationship. At these times, both the parent and their children are left to wonder what really happened.

When one parent lies or exaggerates about the other parent and their actions, it can distort and ruin the positive image the children have of that parent. For the children, it can be incredibly destabilizing when they realize they cannot trust their parents to be truthful at this time, which can lead to them having doubts, insecurities, anxiety, and trust issues with their parents and the situation. This can be particularly confusing if their parents have stressed the importance of truth and honesty within the family.

To ensure the children's emotional and mental well-being is prioritized, it's important to provide information about the reasons for separation and divorce, if known, in a balanced and age-appropriate manner.

Children are often the innocent victims in a divorce, and in some cases, they can be used as hostages or pawns at the discretion of the custodial parent. At times, the children might be allowed to see their estranged parent, while at other times they may not. This can happen unexpectedly, often without notice or an explanation given to the children or the estranged parent.

Over two decades ago, I experienced this scenario several times as an estranged parent. I would drive nearly two hours to our usual weekly meeting place to visit my two young children. On some occasions, I was informed that my mood, words, or actions during the previous weekend's visit didn't meet the standards set by my ex-partner, therefore I was not allowed to visit with my children that weekend.

So, I was dismissed by my ex and told to drive home and think about how I could be a better and more attentive father for my children.

I was actually fuming at this point, feeling the injustice of this situation and the vengeful nature of her words and actions. However, I came to realize that there was nothing I could do at that point to change her opinion of what she believed had happened or the righteousness of her decision.

I found myself in the very sad and vulnerable position that many fathers experience, with no ability to be heard objectively or treated fairly in situations like this. I had painfully come to learn that any complaint from me or outburst of justified angst and frustration would cost me several more weeks of not seeing my children.

Some children may hold onto the hope that their parents will reunite and live together again in the same home. They may pray for this to happen, regardless of how troubled or violent their parents' relationship was. To the child, mom is mom, and dad is dad; the harshness or dysfunctionality of the family doesn't matter, as whatever happened was normal to them.

Life Goes on: Healthy Parenting and Co-Parenting

Separation may bring the challenge of shared parenting, along with the introduction of potential for new partners, girlfriends, or boyfriends into the home. This might include 'special friends' of either parent, who may have sleepovers. Additionally, there is the possibility of blended families, sometimes before the children have had the chance to fully process and get used to their parents' separation.

For parents in new relationships considering moving in together, it is important to give careful consideration and avoid rushing into new living arrangements. Re-partnering and blending families should include plenty of discussion, understanding, compassion, love, and patience for the children from everyone involved.

I have heard of situations where the departing parent had already lined up their next partner at the time of separation. This was a huge shock for the children, who were already overwhelmed from dealing with the significant domestic upheaval and instability caused by the separation.

Next, the children were thrust into a new 'family' situation with hardly any consultation or discussion, and they were expected to happily welcome their parent's new partner and their children into their home and lives.

In situations like this, it is completely understandable that the children may react and struggle to accept their new family configuration. They may quietly grieve in their own way, and any new partner could quickly become a target for their pain and frustration. The children may also, understandably, become angry, tense, argumentative, or dismissive—refusing to play the role of 'happy families', or to share with the new partner and their children.

The sudden change may cause them to experience sleep and eating disorders, as well as stress, confusion, and overwhelm, which can result in a decline in their behavior and grades at school.

It is often said that children are like sponges, resilient and able to absorb changes in their lives. While this is true to a point, children are more like small kitchen sponges than huge car-washing sponges. Therefore, it's essential to consider this when expecting them to easily absorb and adapt to the changes they are forced to accept. Avoid emotionally burdening them with the stress, tension, and scary details that separation and divorce bring to the family dynamic.

Also, the children may find themselves spending time between two very different family structures: their usual home and whatever living arrangement their other parent has been able to create for them.

These are obviously stressful times for the parents as well. Children can register love from their parents based on the amount of quality time they get to spend together. Stressed-out separating parents, who are racing from pillar to post to get everything done, may lose sight of this important detail.

Children love and thrive on quality, unhurried time with their parents. They need to be reassured that things will work out and that they are safe and included in their parents' new living arrangements and life changes.

Parenting and co-parenting work best when everyone involved, parents, new partners, and extended family support members, genuinely value the mental, physical, and emotional health and well-being of the children affected by the separation.

Ideally, the separated parents would demonstrate to their children that they are capable of healthy communication and interactions, including polite and respectful conversations, messaging, and behavior toward each other. They would also be open and flexible with co-parenting timelines, agreements for changeovers, holidays, and special requests.

The Learning Curves of Life

When we invest in creating a healthy, loving home, with clear boundaries for our children, it can become a strong foundation for their whole life.

This means that, even if their parents have separated or divorced, the children will still know they are loved and included in both their parents' new lives.

Children also learn that sometimes friendships and marriages do not work out and come to an end, and that change is a normal part of life. This teaches children that, no matter how much you love someone, if that person doesn't feel the same, then the friendship or relationship can end. This realization can be an important lesson for a child.

Children will also cope better knowing that not all of their friends will always be friendly, as their own circumstances and values change. Adjusting to these changes can sometimes make them feel sad, left out, rejected, or abandoned.

They may come to understand that this period of their life included the wonderful friendship of that person, but that time has moved on and things have changed. They can enjoy the memories and feel happy that they shared those moments together, like chapters in a book.

As with many things in life, there are no guarantees that everything will go as we hope for or plan, or that the people we love will live a long life and remain in our lives. There will be times when a grandparent, relative, favorite pet, or someone else special to them becomes sick and passes away. They will feel sad, cry, and eventually, be able to move on with their lives.

Parents can help children develop important skills, such as navigating challenges and changes, and understanding that feeling sad or grieving is an important and natural part of life. This helps children to learn how to adapt to change and create new connections and new plans when necessary.

Life then becomes a kind of relay race, where you understand that sometimes you have to run the race on your own, and at other times, you are supported by a team of people who help you to reach the next stage of your journey. Just like in the movies, some people will be prominent stars, while others will play smaller roles, yet all are important for the role they play and for the contributions they make to your life.

Extreme Separation Situations

Unfortunately, some people find themselves in horrific and violent situations. Partners who hold extreme and controlling perspectives about how their partner and family should behave can become angry, obsessive, and violent when circumstances do not go according to their wishes. In these situations, the other partner and children can become prisoners in their own home.

Children who grow up in unstable, abusive, and violent homes can be exposed to disturbing displays of physical, mental, emotional, and psychological actions that can haunt them for the rest of their lives.

Some partners of these aggressive individuals may reluctantly choose to tolerate this controlling abusive behavior because they fear the consequences for themselves and their children if they attempt to, or manage to, leave their partner.

In extreme cases, for the protection of the mother and children, they may be helped to leave their home and partner by the police, government, or social support agencies. Unfortunately, being removed from the home and placed in 'secure' housing will not always be enough to guarantee the safety of the mother and her children.

This can create a disruptive cycle for the mother and the children, who are exposed to emergency shelters, short-term living arrangements, new towns, new schools, foster homes, and plenty of uncertainty that they must cope with.

These pressures on the children's mind can cause them to struggle with the stress of changing schools, attempting to fit in, making new friends, and adapting to new living situations. This can affect their grades and their ability to focus in class.

The children can be preoccupied with concerns about their father and when they may be able to see him again. In some intense and sad situations, they may be afraid to see their father due to concerns about how he might react toward their mother, and possibly towards them as well.

Feelings a Child May Experience Based on the Topics Shared in This Chapter

The negative feelings a child can experience when dynamics within the family change include:

Stressed, Tense, Pressured, Worried, Concerned, Deceived, Angry, Betrayed, Dishonest, Vulnerable, Disrespected, Dismissed, Excluded.

Summary

1. Separation and divorce introduce stress and adjustment challenges and can cause children to worry about their parents' well-being.

2. It is essential to protect children from being exposed to negative emotions and verbal abuse between parents.

3. Divorce can lead to children feeling confused and uncertain, and parents should be honest with the children in an age-appropriate manner, avoiding resentment and manipulation.

4. Children often struggle with sudden family changes, like new partners or blended families, after separation.

5. Healthy co-parenting involves clear communication, mutual respect, and prioritizing the children's physical and emotional well-being.

6. Extreme cases of domestic violence and abuse cause severe trauma for children, affecting their emotional and psychological well-being.

4

CHILD BULLYING, EXPLOITATION, AND ONLINE SAFETY

"The challenge in life is not to avoid pain, but to learn how to transform it into wisdom."
— Chuck Spezzano,
The Psychology of Vision

Content Warning

I have taken great care to be sensitive with the information I am presenting here. This chapter contains material that some readers may find distressing or triggering, as it focuses on topics such as bullying, including racial bullying, disability bullying, cyber-bullying, sexual abuse and harassment, forced restriction, physical, emotional, and psychological abuse, confusion, overwhelm, depression, self-harm, and the possibility of suicide.

The stress from many of these topics causes significant issues for the children who are experiencing them, with implications for the teenagers and adults they grow to become.

As a therapist for over twenty years, I have had clients come to see me for a specific issue, often for us to uncover deeper, more traumatic issues and experiences that were the real underlying cause of their concerns. Once these issues were identified and then tapped through, it brought significant benefits to the client.

Similarly, the Targeted EFT process presented in Part Two: The Workbook is designed to help a child and children in the same way.

Bullying and Its Origins

As adults, we know that bullying can happen in many areas of life. It is present in relationships, families, businesses, workplaces, sports, and community groups, politics and more.

Bullying originates in the mind of a selfish person who chooses to take advantage of, control, ridicule, intimidate, or manipulate another person, group, or situation.

In the home, when a parent feels stressed, frustrated, or overwhelmed, and they choose to react to the pressure with angry outbursts, financial constraint, or physical abuse, these bullying actions can leave their partner and children feeling unsafe, nervous, and anxious.

Parents, family members, and others who use bullying behavior to get their needs met become unhealthy, negative role models for their children. Children exposed to these negative bullying displays may mimic the words, actions, or behavior they observe, thinking it will help them get their needs met or improve their chances of survival.

Challenges With Social Interaction for Children at School

Attending school introduces children to a whole new environment where they must adjust to teachers, classmates, school rules, and routines. For many children, school represents the most structured and controlled setting they have ever experienced. While these rules are designed to ensure the safety of the students, teachers, and staff, while also meeting the school's educational and legal obligations, they can also be a source of stress for children adjusting to the environment.

While most parents will focus on ensuring their child's logistical preparation is in order, so they can start school with minimal fuss, no amount of preparation can guarantee how the child will be accepted in the classroom or school environment. The process of adjusting to the school routine can often cause a child to feel stressed and effect their ability to feel safe, speak up, and integrate. An important phase of a child's school life is learning to make friends, fit in, and feel accepted, and included by the other children.

Many factors contribute to how well children adjust to the school and education system. While some children thrive in the classroom environment, enjoying the social interaction, school subjects, and variety on offer, others may find the social exchanges, group learning environment, and competitiveness stressful. This can lead to them feeling anxious, nervous, awkward, stressed, isolated, and overwhelmed.

Schools often include children from a wide range of races, backgrounds, cultures, countries, financial situations, and physical and mental abilities. Some children may look and dress differently, or have physical, mental, and medical conditions. These differences can sometimes become the focus of negative attention, which may lead to them being teased, targeted, or bullied.

As part of a school's duty of care, there may be a requirement for values education and inclusive messaging that attempt to promote a culture of tolerance, understanding, and respect for personal space, boundaries, cultural inclusivity, and other forms of diversity.

While a school can implement the best anti-bullying policies and display posters outlining how they wish the children to interact, it cannot guarantee that all children will be accepted, included, or treated with respect.

I encourage interested parents, teachers, children, and adults to watch the powerful Australian documentary *The School That Tried to Stop Racism (Australia)*,[8][9] presented by Marc Fennell. This ground-breaking program follows a class of primary school students as they learn how to recognize racial bias and are given practical tools to create awareness, positive change, openness, acceptance, and understanding—in their personal views and responses, for their school, class, and within their families.

Understanding Bullying by Children

Children will be children, and this often entails the playing out of pecking orders. These primitive hierarchies can trigger feelings of unease, fear, stress, vulnerability, and overwhelm in the children who experience them.

Often, bullies will target a child based on factors such as their size, race, gender, class, sexual orientation, religion, physical shape or features, clothing, reactionary response, or simply because they seem weak or like an easy target.

This can include teasing, name calling and insults, spreading rumors, swearing, stalking, silently staring, harassment, and other threatening behaviors. More extreme forms of bullying include stealing from a child, such as taking their money, food, or possessions, or using physical actions like hitting, punching, pinching, pushing, shoving, tripping, spitting on them, blocking access to a toilet,

---

[8] Clickview. (n.d.). *The school that tried to end racism.* https://www.clickview.net/au/primary/series/47058657/the-school-that-tried-to-end-racism-australia

[9] Apple TV. (n.d.). *The school that tried to end racism.* https://tv.apple.com/au/show/the-school-that-tried-to-end-racism

school bus, or area the child intends to use, as well as any other behavior the bully chooses to engage in.

Bullies are often opportunistic and will usually be part of a group, targeting children who are smaller, weaker, or more vulnerable. They typically choose moments when the victim has no protective adults or witnesses to intervene, or cameras around to capture their behavior. This can occur on school grounds, bus stops, in shopping centers, or even in neighborhoods.

Bullying interferes with the victimized child's ability to think clearly and feel safe, restricting their freedom in daily life. At school, it can lead to a child and children being afraid to leave the classroom, hiding in the library, and fear being in the school playground at lunchtime. In some situations, bullying behavior in schools can go on for years.

Sometimes, when children grow up and become bigger and stronger, they may become bullies themselves as a way to vent the old hurts, suppressed anger, and frustration from what they experienced. This can often happen at the expense of their partners, family, and others. It may also be seen as a precursor to them becoming a narcissist.[10]

Cyberbullying: A Growing Problem

It would be easy for a parent to believe that the majority of children who experience cyberbullying live in big cities or overseas.

However, the reality is this: the device a predator needs to connect with a child—to gain their attention, interest, and trust—is likely to be within their reach 24 hours a day. As long as their phone has a signal, the child becomes a potential

---

[10] Luntamo, A. H. M., et al. (2020). *Bullying Perpetration and Narcissistic Personality Traits across Adolescence: Joint Trajectories and Childhood Risk Factors*. Frontiers in Psychiatry. https://www.frontiersin.org/journals/psychiatry/articles/10.3389/fpsyt.2020.483229/full

candidate and target for a scammer, hacker, or predator attempting to befriend and manipulate them.

Cyberbullying is a relatively recent form of bullying that has increasingly impacted both children and adults over the past two decades. UNICEF defines cyberbullying as *"…bullying with the use of digital technologies. It can take place on social media, messaging platforms, gaming platforms and mobile phones. It is repeated behavior, aimed at scaring, angering or shaming those who are targeted."*[11]

Cyberbullying can involve a range of harmful behaviors, including attempts to befriend, engage, seduce, harass, belittle, control, intimidate, manipulate, extort money, and more.

Its increase is linked to the easy access and availability of online social media and gaming platforms, which often provide unregulated spaces where adults, teenagers, and children can communicate and leave comments for one another.[12] [13]

Children now have digital access to the world through computers at school and at home, as well as via smartphones, tablets, and smartwatches. Schoolwork often extends beyond school hours, with devices being used for research, assignments, lessons, and more.

While this expanded access provides children with more opportunities for learning, it also increases their exposure to the potential risks of harassment and

---

[11] UNICEF. (n.d.). *Cyberbullying: What is it and how to stop it. A 9-steps guide for parents.* https://www.unicef.org/lac/en/parenting-lac/security-protection/cyberbullying-what-is-how-stop-guide-parents?

[12] Natterhub. (n.d.). *Platform advice.* https://natterhub.com/platform-advice

[13] Willets, M. (2024, July 16). *Keeping kids safe when playing Roblox or Minecraft.* Parents. https://www.parents.com/keeping-kids-safe-on-roblox-or-minecraft-8678099

cyberbullying—at any time of day or night, and often in spaces at home or elsewhere that are not easily monitored by parents or teachers.

Protecting Kids Online: The Need for Regular Parental Supervision

Many parents may feel overwhelmed by what they need to know to keep their children safe online, and hope they can rely on their children to do the right thing.

With school projects, mobile phones, apps, games, social media, and messaging platforms all part of the mix, it is easy to assume that a few good conversations, alongside some parental controls, will do the job. But as children grow and change, so too do the online risks they face.

Each new stage in a child's development brings fresh opportunities for curiosity—and for potential exposure to topics they may not yet be ready to handle. The internet can be a source of learning and laughter, but it also holds real dangers: cyberbullying, predators, scams, and age-inappropriate content, as previously mentioned.

This is why regular parental supervision matters. Not just a one-off talk or occasional glance over their shoulder, but a consistent, open approach to staying involved.

Children need parental guidance in the digital world just as much as they do in the real one. Checking in regularly helps parents notice subtle shifts in their children's behavior—like moodiness, withdrawal, or secrecy—that might suggest something is not quite right, beyond the usual range of teenage moody expressions. These moments give parents the chance to step in early, provide support, and help children process experiences that might otherwise feel confronting, confusing, or scary.[14]

Why Bedrooms Should Be Device-Free

Letting children use devices in private spaces, like bedrooms or studies, increases the likelihood of secretive behavior. Children may stumble across or be sent inappropriate content—and once it is seen, it cannot be unseen. Savvy children will know how to delete apps or browser history to hide what they have been watching. That is why establishing an 'open device use' policy in the home is a must.

Experts also recommend setting clear rules around screen time, app downloads, and who children are allowed to chat with on their phones and online. These rules should be discussed and agreed upon with your children so that expectations are understood and reinforced.[15] [16] [17]

How to Monitor: Tips That Work

- Establish healthy digital habits and rules.

- Set timeframes for mobile phone use.

- Remove mobile phones and devices from the children's bedrooms at night.

---

[14] Inman Grant, J. (2019, August 15). *How to model good screen practices for your child.* https://www.esafety.gov.au/newsroom/blogs/how-to-model-good-screen-practices-for-your-child

[15] eSafety Commissioner. (2025, January 6). *Good habits start young.* https://www.esafety.gov.au/parents/issues-and-advice/good-habits-start-young

[16] eSafety Commissioner. (2024, October 9). *Screen time: How much is too much?* https://www.esafety.gov.au/parents/issues-and-advice/screen-time

[17] Barnardo's. (2019, February 4). *Follow these 5 tips to keep your child safe online.* https://www.barnardos.org.uk/blog/tips-to-keep-your-child-safe-online

- Require devices to be used only in shared spaces (i.e., lounges, kitchens, dining rooms).

- Talk to your children about their online conversations and interactions.

- Require your approval for all app downloads.

- Install parental controls and content filters.

- Randomly check their browser history and app use.

- Review their YouTube topics and other platform usage.

While this may feel intrusive, it is better to risk a child being annoyed at you, than to allow harm to come to them from inappropriate harmful content or comments, cyberbullying, exploitation, and other forms of threats, abuse, and toxicity.[18] [19]

Online Predators and Sextortion: What Parents Need to Know

Predators are increasingly sophisticated. Sextortion—where a child is blackmailed using sexual images, they were tricked into sending—is on the rise. Detective Richard Wistocki is a 30-year Police Detective from Naperville, Illinois, USA, with 20 years of experience as an Internet Crimes Investigator. He is also a founding member of the Illinois Attorney General's High Tech Crimes Bureau (ICAC).

---

[18] NSPCC Learning. (2024, January 11). *Preventing online harm and abuse.* https://learning.nspcc.org.uk/online-safety/preventing-online-abuse-and-harm

[19] U.S. Department of Homeland Security. (n.d.). *Know2Protect: About the Campaign.* https://www.dhs.gov/know2protect/about

In his 2017 TEDx talk entitled: *Why You Should Be Spying on Your Kids*[20], Detective Wistocki speaks of his work in computer crime and online child protection. He shares a sobering fact in child exploitation cases:

"The common denominator in all my sextortion child exploitation cases...is when the parent allows [their child] to charge their devices in their rooms at night, you're sleeping, they shut the door so you can't hear them. It's not a matter of talking, it's typing, reading, and performing with apps like Chromebook, which they get from school...Google Hangouts, Ovoo, Omegle, Skype."

No child is immune. Even children from caring homes can be manipulated or tricked.

Understanding Your Legal Responsibilities

In some cases, parents or guardians can be held legally accountable if children use their devices to harm others—such as sharing non-consensual images, accessing illegal content, or cyberbullying other children. Ignorance is not a defense. Staying informed and involved is essential to meet your responsibilities as a digital-age parent. [21]

Support and Resources

Protecting children in their digital life can feel overwhelming, but their safety, wellbeing, and future are worth every conversation, every limit set, and every app reviewed. With consistent supervision, clear boundaries, and open communication, parents can help their children safely navigate their online world.

---

[20] Wistocki, R. (2017, November). *Why You Should Be Spying on Your Kids*. TEDx Naperville. https://www.ted.com/talks/richard_wistocki_why_you_should_be_spying_on_your_kids

[21] Bartle, J. (2023, June 26). *Accidentally Viewing Child Abuse Material Online*. https://www.criminaldefencelawyers.com.au/blog/accidentally-viewing-child-abuse-material-online

There will be organizations in your area or country that provide guides for parents and children, including tips for setting up devices safely and advice on how to talk to children about online issues and safety.

Police departments and schools will also be likely to offer cyber-safety talks to support families. If you are unsure where to start, speak with your child's school or search the topics online for guidance.

Fear, Intimidation, Bullying, Depression and Overwhelm: The Factors Contributing to Suicide

As a society, we cannot ignore that global statistics have highlighted several key factors contributing to suicide among children and teenagers. [22] [23] [24]

These include stress and overwhelm from mental health disorders, bullying and cyberbullying, family conflict, social isolation and loneliness, alcohol and substance abuse, exposure to violence, harassment, sexual abuse and violation, academic pressure, challenges related to sexual orientation and gender identity,

---

[22] Campisi, S. C., Carducci, B., Akseer, N., Zasowski, C., Szatmari, P., & Bhutta, Z. A. (2020). *Suicidal behaviours among adolescents from 90 countries: a pooled analysis of the Global School-based Student Health Survey.* BMC Public Health, 20, 1102. https://bmcpublichealth.biomedcentral.com/counter/pdf/10.1186/s12889-020-09209-z.pdf

[23] Kim, S., Park, J., Lee, H., Lee, H., Woo, S., Kwon, R., Kim, S., Koyanagi, A., Smith, L., Rahmati, M., Fond, G., Boyer, L., Kang, J., Lee, J. H., Oh, J., & Yon, D. K. (2024). *Global public concern of childhood and adolescence suicide: a new perspective and new strategies for suicide prevention in the post-pandemic era.* World Journal of Pediatrics, 20(7), 872–900. https://link.springer.com/article/10.1007/s12519-024-00828-9

[24] Davey, M. (2024, August 14). *'Alarming' surge in mental ill health among young people in face of 'unprecedented' challenges, experts warn.* The Guardian. https://www.theguardian.com/society/article/2024/aug/14/alarming-surge-in-mental-ill-health-among-young-people-in-face-of-unprecedented-challenges-experts-warn?

romantic rejection, racial, cultural or religious pressures, and digital media influence including social media, apps, websites, and AI tools. [25] [26] [27]

It is important for parents to notice changes in their children, their habits, mannerisms, conversations, and energy, as some of these issues can come on suddenly due to the topics mentioned above. [28] [29]

This can be made easier when children and parents have open dialogue. When children feel safe enough to talk about their stress, concerns, and pressures in their lives, they are more likely to reach out before things spiral out of control for them.

Without the vigilance of parents to recognize the warning signs and respond with patience, sensitivity, and care, it can become very difficult for a child to cope with their thoughts and feelings on their own. Honest and open communication between the child and their parents combined with support from doctors and health professionals can help when issues arise.

---

[25] American Psychological Association. (2023, July). *Psychologists are working to prevent teen suicide*. Monitor on Psychology. https://www.apa.org/monitor/2023/07/psychologists-preventing-teen-suicide

[26] Fraser, H. (2024, October 31). *Deaths linked to chatbots show we must urgently revisit what counts as 'high-risk' AI*. Queensland University of Technology. https://www.qut.edu.au/news/realfocus/deaths-linked-to-chatbots-show-we-must-urgently-revisit-what-counts-as-high-risk-ai

[27] Harrison Dupré, M. (2025, March 20). *Google-backed chatbot platform caught hosting AI impersonations of 14-year-old user who died by suicide*. Yahoo News UK. https://uk.news.yahoo.com/google-backed-chatbot-platform-caught-140358670.html?

[28] Kaslow, N. (2024, September 12). *Teen suicides: What are the risk factors?* Child Mind Institute. https://childmind.org/article/teen-suicides-risk-factors/

[29] Sigel, E. J., & Rahmandar, M. H. (2024, November 4). *Suicide prevention: 12 things parents can do*. HealthyChildren.org. https://www.healthychildren.org/English/healthy-living/emotional-wellness/Pages/suicide-prevention-things-parents-can-do.aspx

Unfortunately, for many children, it can feel unsafe or difficult for them to trust and speak up about their struggles, especially if they have grown up in a family with instability, poor communication and unhealthy parental role models.

In these cases, children may reach out to someone they do trust, like a school nurse, teacher, or a relative, for the support and guidance they need.

Other Schooling Options, Including Home Schooling

When a child is struggling with school— due to not fitting in, bullying, or other issues—they may become sad, stressed, upset, anxious, afraid, and refuse to return to class and the school.

For parents who feel their child is not being treated safely, being accepted, or included in their current school, they may consider transferring them to another, hopefully more supportive school.

In some cities, alternative educational systems such as Steiner, Montessori, or other schools, possibly with a religious foundation, could provide a better fit for the child.

In the US, there are several virtual or online public schools available, while in Australia, students can access a variety of virtual education options, including government-supported distance education programs, private online schools, and *School of the Air* for those in remote areas.

Homeschooling can be another good option, though it does require a significant commitment from the parents, as they take on the teaching role and manage the necessary time, resources, and financial expenses that it involves.

For those parents who choose homeschooling, it is a decision made to prioritize and support the mental, emotional and physical health and well-being of their children. Homeschooling associations around the world offer a wide range of physical and online resources that parents and children can access and benefit from. [30] [31]

Homeschooling also gives parents greater control over what activities their children explore and study, as well as who interacts with them and has access to them.

For my own children, who grew up in the 2000s, homeschooling was our happy choice. We did encounter fearmongers, including a few relatives, who at the time assured us that our decision was 'harming' our children's futures and that attending university would never be an opportunity for them.

Now in their twenties, my children have grown into being strong, independent thinkers with excellent values, communication, and interaction skills. Both of them, having never spent a day in a traditional classroom, have pursued higher education, with one currently studying at university. Homeschooling is not an option for everyone, but for our family it was a great decision.

If you are considering homeschooling, virtual, or alternative education systems for your children, be brave, explore your options, and do what is best for both you and your children at the time —without fear or guilt. This decision will require time, care, planning, energy, lifestyle changes, and commitment to manage successfully.

Be personally involved in your children's education and healthy developmental activities; they will come to love and appreciate you and your efforts, eventually.

---

[30] Home Education Association, Inc. (n.d.). *Home Education Association Australia.* https://www.hea.edu.au/

[31] Home School Legal Defense Association. (n.d.) *Home School Legal Defense Association.* https://hslda.org/

Adolescence on Netflix 2025: A Wake-Up Call for Parents

Just as we were completing the final draft of this book, the British four-part TV series *Adolescence*[32] aired on Netflix. At the time of writing, it had become one of the most-watched shows on Netflix, ranking number four on the all-time top ten list.

Adolescence is a dramatized story of a 13-year-old boy whose romantic advances were rejected both online and in person by a girl he liked at school.

The story showed the boy and his pubescent male friends as they attempted to navigate the confusing world of boy-girl relationships—a phase many people will remember in their own lives as a challenging time occasionally filled with rejection and embarrassment.

But unlike a typical Hollywood coming-of-age tale, this story took a tragic and violent turn when the boy was rejected and publicly shamed by the girl. He felt angry, embarrassed, and humiliated, and planned his retaliation with his friends—ultimately choosing to murder her.

The story unfolds through the lens of a police investigation, which was swift and effective due to CCTV footage that captured the murder. Rather than focusing solely on the crime, the series explores and reveals the motivations and negative influences that led to the boy's actions, as well as the devastating impact on his family, her family, the school and schoolchildren, and the wider community.

As mentioned, the events leading to the murder began with the boy's romantic advances being rejected by the girl. The police investigation revealed that, in several social media posts on the boy's account, the girl used comments and

---

[32] *Adolescence*. (2025). *Netflix*. https://www.netflix.com

rejection-themed emojis that referred to him as an 'incel' (involuntarily celibate),[33] suggesting he was too unattractive to be liked or dated.

The modern use of the term incel, refers to individuals, primarily heterosexual men, who feel unable to form romantic or sexual relationships with women, despite wanting to do so. It is also associated with online communities, referred to as the 'manosphere',[34] where boys and men express their frustration, anger, and resentment, toward women—whom they often blame for their romantic disappointments and perceived failures.

These negative and hateful beliefs about girls, women, and relationships contribute to the spread of misogyny and violent behavior against girls and women, which is the basis of the story.

My Perspective on Watching *Adolescence*

I certainly felt empathy for this situation as a parent, and it is easy to judge the parents of this boy. The following points include spoilers and are offered to provide further context:

- The parents were unaware that their 13-year-old son was out walking the streets at night with his mates in their town, well after 10.00pm.

- The parents were deeply shocked and struggled to comprehend that their son was capable of such premeditated and extreme violence, which led to the tragic murder of the schoolgirl.

---

[33] Incel. (2025, May 13). *Incel*. Wikipedia. https://en.wikipedia.org/wiki/Incel?

[34] Manosphere. (2025, May 9). *Manosphere*. Wikipedia. https://en.wikipedia.org/wiki/Manosphere

- The father watched the CCTV footage of the murder his son committed and was understandably shocked and stunned by his son's denial of his involvement.

- It became clear that the boy had been heavily influenced by toxic male, misogynistic online communities. It opened my eyes to a world that many parents—and perhaps even their children—will not yet fully understand.

- Much of the storyline followed the parents' emotional journey as they tried to process the shock of this devastating event—a tragedy that changed their lives, as well as the victim's family's lives, and impacted upon many other people in their community.

- The parents found themselves struggling with this tragic event and were seen attempting to convince each other that, despite everything, they were good parents.

- There were unsettling scenes involving a young, attractive female child psychologist who was interviewing the boy accused of murder. On a few occasions, during their time together, the boy lost his temper and became menacingly aggressive, as he taunted and intimidated her and then quickly dropped back into his seemingly innocent, 'cute boy' persona. This sudden change in his mood startled both the child psychologist and the viewing audience.

- The story ended with me and the viewing audience left to ponder about how some people's beliefs, opinions, rants, and hatred on the internet have become so accessible and negatively influential on the minds and actions of young boys and men.

What's New About the Storyline of *Adolescence*?

Unfortunately, there is not much that is new in this story. Adolescence highlights a sadly all too familiar theme that has become more accessible and searchable through the influence of misogynistic content shared on popular social media platforms.

The script and its visual representation brought home, for many parents and families, the shock of how quickly situations can turn tragically wrong. Whether it is verbal abuse that escalates into rejection, anger, bullying, or ends with physical violence.

Adolescence reminds us that early awareness and open, ongoing conversations with the children at home are essential in preventing the ripple effects of unchecked emotional pain and toxic influence.

Were the parents in *Adolescence* paying the price for not being more involved in their son's school life, his thoughts, challenges, perspectives, and feelings?

Maybe. It is a difficult question, but one worth reflecting on.

There are immense pressures on school-aged children—many of which are unspoken by the child, and therefore, not communicated to the parent. This creates a problem: if the parent isn't aware of the issues the child is experiencing, how can they support them?

Creating a safe space for open communication between parents and their children is key to alleviating some of these issues and pressures. While there is no guarantee that children will easily open up and share honestly with their parents, one would hope it is never too late to start.

Parents can begin by taking the time to ask their children about their day and listen to their responses. At times, parents may be shocked by their children's thoughts, questions, or comments. But it is far better to hear and attempt to answer these things in your own home, rather than through the police or in other distressing circumstances.

The parents of the boy in *Adolescence* came across to me as being more interested in talking **at** him rather than **to** him. This was shown to be not an unusual situation as his father was very busy, working long hours in his own business, and had limited time to spend with either of his children.

In this case, the boy's main sources of opinions and information were his school friends, the internet, and toxic masculinity-driven social media influencers that they chose to watch.

School-aged girls are often under pressure from inappropriate sexualized comments and questions from boys and men, which may disturb and embarrass them. They will often talk with their friends about how to respond to these comments. However, the advice shared may not always be suitable, sensible, or ensure their safety.

It may have been conversations like these that influenced how the girl in Adolescence responded to the advances of the boy and others.

My Most Important Message from *Adolescence* for Parents is This

When it comes to protecting our children, we would hope we have advised them well in how to respond and react in most situations. That is why it is important to create open and safe communication in the home, where children feel heard and supported. A child's innocence, self-worth, self-love, self-respect, and peace of mind are priceless—and should be treasured and protected by us, as parents.

Feelings a Child May Experience Based on the Topics Shared in This Chapter

Negative feelings a child or teenager may experience from all forms of bullying include:

Frustration, Anger, Fear, Nervousness, Insecurity, Tension, Stress, Anxiety, Hypervigilance, Being Picked On, Victimized, Targeted, Confused, Teased, Bullied, Violated, Abused, Objectified, Controlled. Traumatized, Overwhelmed, Embarrassed, Ashamed, Humiliated.

Summary

1. Bullying can occur in various areas of life, including in the home, relationships, schools, and workplaces.

2. Bullying often originates from a person's exploitative mindset, aiming to control or manipulate others.

3. Dysfunctional home environments, such as abusive parenting, can introduce children to bullying behaviors.

4. Children can mimic bullying behaviors they see in their homes to gain approval or fulfill their needs.

5. School can be challenging for children, as they must adjust to social interactions, fitting in, making friends and group learning activities.

6. Children are vulnerable to bullying based on physical differences, race, disabilities, online attacks, or other perceived weaknesses.

7. Bullying in schools can range from teasing to physical violence, stealing etc.

8. Cyberbullying is a growing problem, facilitated by easy access to mobile phones, digital devices, and social media.

9. Parents must regularly monitor their children's online activities in the home and enforce safety rules to prevent exploitation.

10. Homeschooling, virtual, or alternatives schools may be an option for children who feel unsafe or excluded in traditional school settings.

11. Open and safe communication in the home, is important for children to feel heard and supported.

5

SEXUAL ABUSE AND VIOLATION TRAUMA

"We cannot change our past, but we can change the meaning of our past."
— John Bradshaw,
Homecoming: Reclaiming and Championing Your Inner Child

Content Warning

I have taken great care to be sensitive with the information I am presenting here. This chapter contains material that some readers may find distressing or triggering, as it addresses topics such as sexual abuse and violation trauma, including physical, emotional, and psychological abuse, harassment, rape, forced restriction, confusion, overwhelm, depression, self-harm, and suicidal thoughts and tendencies.

In an extreme situation where the child has experienced sexual abuse and violation trauma, their immediate care needs to be attended to, which may include medical attention and police involvement.

Sometime after this, the parent may enquire with the child if they feel ready and willing to engage in a Targeted EFT therapy process. The child's consent is required and no actions should be taken until they are ready to participate.

As a therapist for over twenty years, I have had clients come to see me for a specific issue, often for us to uncover deeper, more traumatic issues and experiences that were the real underlying cause of their concerns. Once these issues were identified and then tapped through, it brought significant benefits to the client.

*Similarly, the Targeted EFT process presented in **Part Two: The Workbook** can help a child in the same way.*

Please be aware that the conscious survival-focused mind can attempt to block, sometimes for decades, any memory of sexual abuse, violation, or trauma experienced by them as a child or teenager.

Defining Sexual Abuse and Violation Trauma

One of the most surprising realizations for me as a therapist has been discovering just how many of my adult clients have experienced sexual abuse in their childhood, teenage, and adult years.

Sexual abuse, violation, rape and the traumatic implications from these intense and overwhelming experiences are, unfortunately, not new topics for women, girls, and to a lesser degree some men and boys in society. I suspect this has actually been a reality for people since the beginning of mankind. A thought that many people in modern societies may prefer to never think about or believe could be true.

In the early 2000s, I developed definitions for sexual abuse and violation trauma that I have found to be both accurate and very helpful for assisting my adult clients identify and relate to their experiences.

Definitions of Sexual Abuse and Violation Trauma for my Adult Clients:

1. Hearing and being exposed to sleazy, disrespectful, inappropriate comments, text messages, suggestions, propositions, and harassment.

2. Feeling that you have been inappropriately touched, handled, brushed, grabbed or tickled at any age.

3. Being flashed at or sent or shown explicit images.

4. Feeling that you have been disrespected sexually including being coerced, intoxicated or drugged, and touched, penetrated, or raped by a known or unknown person, or in a relationship or marriage.

In some cases, when my clients heard these definitions, their views changed about how they felt about certain experiences and relationships they have had across their lives. For many women, some of these experiences happened decades ago, when the definitions I present here were considered to be normal and acceptable behavior.

Sadly, these descriptions can also be used to define the types of sexual abuse and violation that some children and teenagers have or may experience as well.

The Impact of Pornography on School-Aged Children

In modern times, it can be difficult for young teenagers and teenagers to adjust to the wide range of expectation and distorted beliefs they have about what love, sex, and relating means.

In some situations, these areas of relating and connecting for young guys and girls has become confusing and murky due to the accessibility and exposure to porn sites, erotic music videos, movies, advertising, social media influencers, and apps like SnapChat, all accessible via their smartphones.

This exposure can be a contributing factor to school-aged children who feel pressured by their peer group to engage in certain sexual activities with FOMO—the Fear of Missing Out. In some cases, participating in these activities can be treated as a right of passage and something to be admired by their school friends. Unfortunately, this is not a new concept.

As a result, some schoolgirls may feel the need to appear sexually confident, available, adventurous, and just experienced enough to gain the attention of boys—many of whom have been influenced by pornography.

Exposure to pornography can lead many immature and delusional boys to develop a perverse and distorted belief that the acts depicted on porn sites reflect the secret desires of schoolgirls and women everywhere.

Schoolchildren who have experienced physical or sexual abuse—whether from schoolboys, teachers, staff, coaches, or other men—will often find themselves feeling nervous, anxious, cautious, abused, violated, shamed, humiliated, depressed, overwhelmed, traumatized, and in some cases, have suicidal thoughts.

In recent years, I have seen several documentaries in Australia highlighting the rise of assaults and sexual abuse involving schoolgirls and schoolboys. These programs also featured that female schoolteachers have been impacted by misogynistic comments and actions from schoolboys, male schoolteachers, and even school administrators.[35][36][37]

---

[35] Milligan, L. (2024, March 14). *The questions that remain for Cranbrook School as new allegations flood in.* ABC News. https://www.abc.net.au/news/2024-03-14/cranbrook-school-new-allegations-four-corners/103587004

[36] Cleal, O. (2024, March 4). *Elite all-boys school Cranbrook under the spotlight with allegations from former female staff members.* Women's Agenda. https://womensagenda.com.au/latest/elite-all-boys-school-cranbrook-under-the-spotlight-with-allegations-from-former-female-staff-members/

[37] Harris, C. (2023, May 12). *Beyond Purity: The Story Behind the Four Corners Investigation.* National Secular Lobby. https://www.nsl.org.au/columns/beyond-purity-the-story-behind-the-four-corners-investigation

Impacts of Sexual Abuse and Violation on a Child or Teenager

The shock of experiencing sexual abuse or violation can turn a vibrant, expressive, outgoing, and confident child into being nervous, anxious, and fearful. From that point on, the child may hold the view that some people are not safe to be around. They may become afraid to leave their room or home or return to school, or take part in sports training or any activities they previously enjoyed.

The child also may be understandably reluctant to return to the place, room, home, or venue where the violation occurred—or continues to occur. This fear becomes more intense for the child if the abuser lives in their home, or visits, especially if the abuser has threatened them to keep silent and not speak up to their parents.

In some cases, I have heard that the abuser forced the child to remain silent about the abuse they were experiencing by threatening to hurt and violate their sister or mother if the child ever spoke up. The fears related to this pressure on the child made them feel like they were a prisoner in their own home, terrified that the abuse will never end. Often, the abuse continued for many years.

My clients have told me that these types of sexual abuse situations for them changed when they felt they had the maturity, mental strength, and courage to speak up and expose the abuser. Or when circumstances changed, such as them leaving the home, or the abuser stopped visiting, moved away, or died.

The Physical, Mental, and Emotional Reactions to Sexual Abuse and Violation

For the child, the shock associated with being held, restricted, detained, touched, or forced to be quiet and comply by a stronger, demanding person or group can be an embarrassing, painful, confusing, overwhelming, and traumatizing experience.

A child may feel shocked, scared, and in pain from the physical restriction and assault they have experienced. It is also likely that the child may have 'dissociated', which is a split of their mental and emotional capacity to cope with what happened to them during the terrifying encounter.

The fear and dissociation may lead to them feeling numb and not having the words or ability to be heard, speak up, and defend themselves.

After the traumatic event, the child's mind would have done its best to ensure their survival and to find a way for them to carry on. In some cases, the child will never tell anyone about the abuse or violation they have experienced.

While they may look the same as before the violation, they are no longer the same person. As a result of the violation, the child may display a complete change in their personality including the way they interact, feel, speak, and present themselves. They might appear as reclusive, quiet, sad, anxious, depressed, and numb from the shock, confusion, anger, and betrayal they felt. As they grow, the anxiety they carry may lead to increased stress, tension, anger, aggression, and impatience—both with themselves and others.

They may also experience insomnia and begin weeping at random times, avoid sleeping in their own bed, experience bed-wetting, depression, panic attacks, excessive bathing, mental health issues, self-mutilation, cutting, suicidal thoughts or attempts, etc. caused by fear, flashbacks, or recurring nightmares.

Coping at Home After the Sexual Abuse of a Child

No matter how much parents would hope and wish that their child will be okay after experiencing sexual abuse and violation trauma, the reality is, in my opinion, the child will never be the same again. The guilt parents may feel because of this may never end either, and they may punish themselves for not being able to foresee the threat and protect their child from the abuser.

Some parents may attempt to deal with their feelings of anger, guilt, grief and powerlessness, etc., by attempting to seek justice for what has happened to their child. The parents may become overprotective and hypervigilant with strict rules and requirements for their children, by imposing tight security measures that keep everyone in the family on edge.

The topic of their child's sexual abuse can create awkward conversations in the home, as the parents attempt to sensitively inquire about how their child is feeling and whether there is anything they need or would like to say.

This can also be difficult for the child as they attempt to make sense of the abuse they endured and find ways to mentally and emotionally cope with and integrate the new feelings of fear, anxiety, and depression that sometimes overwhelm them.

Some parents may be in such pain, denial, and overwhelm that they refuse to acknowledge or discuss the sexual abuse their child experienced, even with the child. As a result, it becomes a taboo topic that is not spoken of within the family.

In some situations, an abused child may receive pressure from their parents and family members to *never speak* about the sexual abuse they experienced. This can often be the case when the abuser is a known family member, relative, friend, or respected elder in the community.

The pressure of remaining silent and denying the abuse can intensify the child's physical and emotional pain, anger, confusion, and frustration due to the betrayal, lack of support, and the alienation they felt from their family.

This decision by the parents does not help their confused, frightened, and vulnerable child to feel safe, loved, or supported, making it even harder for the child to accept help to heal from the traumas they have experienced.

Part of what makes the topic of sexual abuse so challenging for people to talk about is that statistically speaking, it is so prevalent in society. And it is very likely that the child's own parents, siblings, or people known to them have experienced some form of sexual abuse or violation trauma themselves in their own childhood, teenage, or adult years. Whether they acknowledge it or not is another matter.

To help the child recover from sexual abuse and violation trauma, the parents need to provide a safe space and opportunities for the child to speak up whenever they feel sad, nervous, triggered, afraid, depressed, or insecure.

Feelings a Child May Experience Based on the Topics Shared in This Chapter

The negative feelings a child or teenager may experience from all forms of abuse include:

Restricted, Touched, Coerced, Abused, Violated, Disrespected, Angry, Embarrassed, Enraged, Bullied, Set Up, Betrayed, Controlled, Manipulated, Shocked, Tense, Suspicious, Hypervigilant, Traumatized, Damaged, Unclean, Guilty, Responsible, Rejected, Abandoned, Helpless, Hopeless, Depressed, Overwhelmed.

Summary

1. Sexual abuse and violation trauma are widespread issues that affect both children, teenagers, and adults, with long-lasting effects.

2. Abuse includes verbal harassment, inappropriate physical contact, exposure to explicit images, bullying and cyberbullying, penetration, coercion, non-consent, rape, and more.

3. Children who experience abuse may become fearful, anxious, and withdrawn, and struggle to live, interact and function at school and in their daily activities.

4. Abuse can lead to physical pain, shock, and emotional dissociation, depression and overwhelm.

5. Family members can struggle with supporting an abused child, leading to tension, denial, or silence around the abuse.

6. Healing requires time, support, and space for children to express themselves and navigate their emotions.

7. The Targeted EFT process can be effective in helping children cope with trauma and feel safer in their lives.

CONCLUSION

Moving Forward with Care and Confidence

The topics covered in Part One highlight the range and intensity of emotional wounds that children may carry. Gaining an understanding of these issues can help the facilitator to prepare and support the child with compassion and clarity, and the tools they will need to deliver the Targeted EFT process.

We now move on to the practical steps and guidance needed to do this. This begins with understanding the facilitator's role and responsibilities—how to create a safe, respectful, and effective healing space for the child.

Even if you are new to this kind of support work, the process has been written to help parents, teachers, and caring adults to step into the facilitator's role.

**PART TWO:
THE WORKBOOK**

6

FACILITATOR'S ROLE AND RESPONSIBILITIES

Who Can Be a Facilitator?

A facilitator of the Targeted EFT process presented in this book can be a parent, grandparent, stepparent, foster parent, relative, trusted family friend, schoolteacher, school counsellor, teacher aide, youth worker, social worker, therapist, or any other caring and safe adult.

The facilitator is someone with compassionate communication skills, a kind heart, and a patient, supportive manner. Most importantly, they are a safe and trustworthy person.

If a caring adult would like to be a facilitator, they need to have the appropriate credentials confirming they are safe to work with children (such as a completed police check or equivalent).

For example, in Queensland, Australia—where I live—a person is required to obtain a 'Blue Card' to work with children. This involves a police check conducted by the Department of Justice and Attorney-General (Blue Card Services)[38]. This process includes checking a person's history for any criminal history, pending charges, past convictions, disciplinary information from professional bodies, sex

---

[38] Queensland Government. (n.d.). *Blue Card*. https://www.qld.gov.au/law/laws-regulated-industries-and-accountability/queensland-laws-and-regulations/regulated-industries-and-licensing/blue-card-services

offender registers, child protection offender orders, and any domestic violence information.

For prospective facilitators, please check for the requirements that apply in your state, region, or country.

What is the Facilitator's Role?

The facilitator's role is to learn and deliver the Targeted EFT process as presented in this book. They may choose to make themselves available to work with schools or parents in supporting children through the Tapping process. This includes determining their suitability with a child's parents to support the child's specific issues.

From there, they organize consent forms (particularly for school-based Tapping sessions), and arrange the details including date, time, and location.

It is up to the facilitator whether they choose to charge a fee, which may cover their time and travel expenses, or they may choose to donate their time. If the facilitator is charging a fee, it should be agreed upon between the facilitator and the child's parent(s) or the school at the time of arranging the Tapping session.

We will soon be offering certified training courses in Targeted EFT, which will include how to deliver sessions for children, teenagers, and adults. Graduates will be eligible to charge for their services as Certified Facilitators of Targeted EFT.

Facilitator Check List for a Home or School-Based Tapping Session

Check lists have been prepared for both home and school-based Tapping sessions, with the links to download them available in the **Resources** section.

The Facilitator's Statement of Intention

As well as having the genuine desire to help children, I feel that it is important to have a positive, kind, open, and patient mindset when working with children.

I have prepared a **Statement of Intention** to help the facilitator (even if they are a parent) to be in a good head and heart space to support a child with the Tapping process.

It offers a reminder to have compassionate detachment so that you can be present and patient when you support the child.

"I offer my best intentions, patience, focus, and energy to help (name of the child) today. My intention is to support and strengthen their head and heart balance, so they can feel safer, cope better, speak up, and achieve well in their life."

Why Parental Consent is Important

Parental consent is important to ensure that parents understand and agree to the reasons why a Targeted EFT session is being offered to their child.

The **Parental Consent Form** includes the following key points:

- The parents understand that the purpose of the Tapping session is to help their child feel better.

- They acknowledge that no specific outcomes are guaranteed.

- They are aware that the facilitator will conduct the session with professional care and respect.

- It is suggested that they sit in the room with their child during the session.

An example of a **Parental Consent Form** is provided in the **Resources** section and may be adapted by the facilitator to suit their needs. Once signed and dated, the facilitator should file the form for future reference.

7

PREPARING A CHILD FOR TARGETED EFT

A one-to-one Targeted EFT session for a child takes about 30 minutes. Prior to the Tapping process, the facilitator selects the most appropriate Tapping statements (featured in Chapter 8) for the issues affecting the child.

The Targeted EFT Tapping statements are used with the Tapping process (featured in Chapter 10). This combination helps a child by identifying, acknowledging, and providing the words to describe the stressful issues that have made them feel sad, scared, nervous, anxious, stressed, confused, depressed, overwhelmed etc.

The facilitator reads the selected Tapping statement aloud while tapping specific acupressure points on themselves. The child then repeats the statement and taps the points on themselves as demonstrated by the facilitator. This combination activates an overriding sequence in the child's mind to reduce the stressful issues and deliver the positive changes necessary to help them.

There are usually three to four statements tapped through during the session, followed by two Completion statements (explained in Chapter 10) to finish and anchor the positive changes made within the session.

Some children, after benefiting from a session, have asked for another when they begin to feel stressed, anxious, or overwhelmed.

A teacher can also facilitate a Tapping session to help boost students' attention, focus, mental clarity, and retention of information. It can also support their emotional and mental health, and well-being.

Positive results from tapping with children were observed and reported by Margaret Lambert, Ph.D., who conducted a study for her thesis called *The Tapping Project: Introducing Emotional Freedom Techniques (EFT) to Reduce Anxiety and Improve Wellbeing in Primary School Students*,[39] published in May 2020.

One teacher, Maria, shared her experience: *".... after a week, they* [the students] *were like: "Miss, we've got to do tapping!"* Another teacher, Sheila added, *"Yeah, they were really eager to do it. They were like, in the morning: "We've gotta do tapping before we do anything else.'"* Maria also noted, *"...they would remind me if I forgot."* [40]

I have provided a link to more details about this study in the **Resource** section.

There are other versions of tapping being used to help children in schools internationally with great benefits.

Identifying a Child Who Can Benefit from Targeted EFT

There are many children who may benefit from a Targeted EFT session due to their personal issues, social challenges, family or domestic circumstances, or from a range of upsetting situations they may have experienced.

---

[39] Lambert, M. T. (2020). *The Tapping Project: Introducing Emotional Freedom Techniques (EFT) to reduce anxiety and improve wellbeing in primary school students*. (Master's thesis, Charles Darwin University, 2020). Charles Darwin University Research Repository. https://ris.cdu.edu.au/ws/portalfiles/portal/35605489/Thesis_CDU_35605334_Lambert_M.pdf

[40] Lambert, M. T. (2020). *The Tapping Project: Introducing Emotional Freedom Techniques (EFT) to reduce anxiety and improve wellbeing in primary school students*. (Master's thesis, Charles Darwin University), p. 199. Charles Darwin University Research Repository. https://ris.cdu.edu.au/ws/portalfiles/portal/35605489/Thesis_CDU_35605334_Lambert_M.pdf

For many children, their schoolteachers and teacher aides may be the only adults they know and trust outside of their family. Teachers are often kind, accessible, supportive and wise, and have qualities that may not always be present in the child's home due to various health or other issues their parents may be experiencing.

When a child is sad, confused, hurting, or overwhelmed from being stressed, teased, or bullied at school, or from living in a difficult family and domestic situation etc., tapping can be a valuable tool to help them to quickly recover.

Children's minds can be very subjective, often viewing their lives in a black and white fashion. They may see themselves as either winning or losing, having a good day or a bad day, being liked and popular or not, being smart or not, and achieving good grades or not.

The child's conscious survival-focused mind will scan their lives for signs that they are loved, safe, supported, and included, as well as the times they do not feel this.

When a child feels judged, criticized, belittled, or shamed by parents, family members, or others, they often will not consider that the person saying these things might be wrong, harsh, or cruel.

Instead, they may interpret the criticism from what they heard to mean they aren't good enough, aren't lovable, aren't smart, or are worthless, which leads to feelings of hopelessness, shame, overwhelm, and depression.

In families that communicate unconsciously and insensitively, the parents and family members can be pessimistic, which may lead to low self-esteem, low self-worth, and communication, and psychological issues for their children. Harsh and critical comments may only need to be said once to a child for their effects to last a lifetime.

Children exposed to these dynamics often struggle to trust and believe in themselves, and may develop speech and learning difficulties, and self-critical beliefs. This can lead to them feeling sad, anxious, and depressed, along with a fear of thinking independently, speaking up, and expressing themselves. This can make them more susceptible to following others and being manipulated by stronger, more controlling individuals.

When a child has a fear of speaking up, it can often be linked to experiences where they were scared, belittled, teased, embarrassed, threatened, hit, hurt, shamed, bullied, oppressed or rejected when they tried to talk, read, sing, or express themselves at home or school.

Signs That a Child May Benefit from the Targeted EFT:

- Experiencing anxiety, fear, or nervousness in family or school situations.

- Displaying sudden changes in behavior, such as mood swings, withdrawal, isolation, depression, or acting out with disrespect and anger.

- Having difficulty concentrating or showing reluctance to talk, interact, or play with other children.

- Being stressed, tense, or hitting other children.

- Expressing overwhelming emotions, such as sadness, anger, frustration, or confusion.

- Being anxious, nervous, teased or bullied.

- Struggling with speaking up and expressing themselves in the classroom.

- Experiencing a recent trauma or loss such as parental divorce, death of a family member or a pet).

When the topics such as fear of speaking up, being scared, or bullied are tapped through in a session, it can help shift the child's energy, allowing them to feel safer, more confident, and courageous. This new level of confidence can positively support other aspects of their life in exciting ways.

8

TARGETED EFT TAPPING STATEMENTS FOR CHILDREN

The Targeted EFT Tapping statements are designed to fit perfectly into the Tapping sequence, to enable the facilitator to easily deliver the Targeted EFT Tapping process to help support children.

The statements are written to represent how a child feels—or may have felt—about the confusing, stressful or traumatic events they have experienced.

I mention this because, in my work as a therapist, I have written over 300 Tapping statements for teenagers and my adult clients that address the more intense and challenging issues they may experience. These statements are not included in this book.

Many of a child's fears and issues have come from their parents, siblings, family members, and the home or life experiences that have scared, frightened, or traumatized them. Children also acquire fears, beliefs, habits, and biases from their parents and other influential people in their lives.

The Tapping statements help by defining the issues that have impacted upon a child—who, in many cases, may lack the vocabulary or presence of mind to understand and express what happened to them. This can be due to their age, the shock and overwhelm from what they have experienced, or a physical or mental condition they suffer from.

The statements have been specifically written to reflect back to the child's conscious survival-focused mind the many negative, limiting, fearful, and overwhelming thoughts and beliefs that it uses against the child in any given moment.

Each statement, when used with the Tapping process, momentarily creates a minor shock within the conscious survival-focused mind as it recognizes that it has been using the same or similar groups of words and feelings to control and manipulate the child.

This momentary 'unlocking of the shock' provides just enough time for the Tapping process to 'unlock the blocks'—disentangling the maze of self-protective mechanisms the mind has set up to prevent itself from being accessed and having its thoughts or beliefs changed.

The Tapping statements help to access and reduce the issues and fears stored within the child's mind. Then, the positive statement of *"I love and accept myself"* is inserted in its place. And just like magic, the negative statement is transformed into being a positive statement and new belief.

It should be acknowledged that the conscious survival focused mind is not a villain. It is a subset of the conscious mind that has been tasked with protecting the child.

It is actually on the child's side and wants the child to succeed and prosper in their life. However, its job description requires it to be hypervigilant, suspicious, alert, and reactive to any and all perceived threats or challenges that may negatively impact or hurt the child.

What Targeted EFT provides the facilitator with is a new and effective way to work with the child's conscious survival-focused mind—to help it be 'spring cleaned' and reset, so it can continue to protect the child while allowing the child to think, feel, communicate, play, and respond better in their life.

Tapping Statements by Category with Explanations

Each Tapping statement is categorized with an alphanumeric code, making it easy for the facilitator to identify and select the most appropriate statements for a Targeted EFT session.

Parents, Siblings, and Family (PSF)

Some parents, due to their priorities, habits, relationship issues, job, financial, health and mental issues, and personal circumstances may struggle, at times, to provide a safe and stable home. In these situations, some children may choose to draw attention to themselves in negative ways—which can also add to them feeling more sad, nervous, anxious, hurt, disappointed, overwhelmed, isolated, rejected, or abandoned.

It is important to understand that these perceptions are shaped by the child's individual perspectives, and this can happen in the most loving and nurturing of families, as well as the most dysfunctional ones. Some of these issues for the child may display themselves in the statements presented here.

The Tapping statements are presented in the exact phrasing I recommend the facilitator use—spoken line by line for the child to repeat after each line during the session. This is done to prevent overwhelming an already stressed child.

Parents, Siblings and Family (PSF)

PSF .1.

Even though
**I feel
sad, unloved, and unimportant
when Mom and Dad
are too busy working
to spend time with me.**
I love and accept myself.

PSF .2.

Even though
**I feel
sad, stressed, and unsafe
when my parents
argue and fight all the time.**
I love and accept myself.

PSF .3.

Even though
**I feel
sad and left out
when my brother / sister,
won't talk to me,
include or play games with me.**
I love and accept myself.

PSF .4.

Even though
**I feel
sad, scared and nervous
when Mom and Dad
can't look after me
and I have to live
with relatives or other people.**
I love and accept myself.

PSF .5.

Even though
**I feel
scared and sad that *…………..
does not live with us anymore,
and I worry about them.**
I love and accept myself.

(*Insert: Dad, Mom or person's name.)

PSF .6.

Even though
**I feel
scared and nervous when *………..,
are drunk and use drugs
and they are angry,
and unsafe to be around.**
I love and accept myself.

(* Insert: Mom, Dad or person's name.)

Upset and Angry (UA)

It is normal, at times, for a child to feel upset, angry, and frustrated, with a strong need to express themselves.

Some children may choose to express their feelings by mimicking the way their parents display anger and frustration. If a parent frequently becomes noisy, angry, aggressive, dismissive, or swears a lot, the child may use those words and behaviors at home, at school, or in public.

The Tapping statements are presented in the exact phrasing I recommend the facilitator use—spoken line by line for the child to repeat after each line during the session. This is done to prevent overwhelming an already stressed child.

Upset and Angry (UA)

UA .1.

Even though
**I feel
stressed and angry
when I get things wrong
at school and home.**
I love and accept myself.

UA .2.

Even though

I feel

frustrated, upset, and angry

when I don't get what I want

I love and accept myself.

UA .3.

Even though

I feel

angry and upset,

when I am not asked

about what I want or need.

I love and accept myself.

UA .4.

Even though

I feel

upset and angry

when I am not picked

for the team /group.

I love and accept myself.

Rejection and Abandonment (RA)

When parents are unable or incapable of managing their parental role, a child may feel nervous, anxious, scared, insecure, and rejected. In these circumstances, the child may experience feelings of rejection and abandonment within their family, among friends, in their neighborhood or social groups, at school, or elsewhere.

The Tapping statements are presented in the exact phrasing I recommend the facilitator use—spoken line by line for the child to repeat after each line during the session. This is done to prevent overwhelming an already stressed child.

Rejection and Abandonment (RA)

RA .1.

Even though
I feel
scared, nervous, anxious,
sad, and lonely.
I love and accept myself.

RA .2.

Even though
I feel
sad, stressed, unhappy,
confused, rejected, and abandoned
I love and accept myself.

RA .3.

Even though

I feel

stressed, ignored, unheard,

confused, lonely, and left out.

I love and accept myself.

RA .4.

Even though

I feel

rejected by kids at school

and I don't know how

to make them like or include me.

I love and accept myself.

Bullying and Conflict (BC)

When a child or children decide to use their words or actions to impose their will and desires onto a vulnerable child or group of children, this behavior is called bullying.

Situations leading to displays of bullying and conflict can appear to happen without warning to the targeted child. Whether on their own or with friends, some children may be picked on, hurt, teased, roughed up, or frightened by a bully.

The bully's goal is to frighten, scare, and intimidate the child into complying with their demands. These demands may include the mental and physical control and humiliation of the targeted child they are picking on, for the bully's own needs and amusement. A bully may also seek to take the child's money, lunch, phone, or other possessions.

The Tapping statements are presented in the exact phrasing I recommend the facilitator use—spoken line by line for the child to repeat after each line during the session. This is done to prevent overwhelming an already stressed child.

Bullying and Conflict (BC)

BC .1.

Even though
**I feel
nervous and uncomfortable,
afraid, and insecure,
when kids are noisy
and rough with me.**
I love and accept myself.

BC .2.

Even though

I feel

scared, judged, angry,

frustrated, and powerless

when kids tease, mock, and bully me.

I love and accept myself.

BC .3.

Even though

I feel

after being picked on and bullied at school,

I am now afraid to go to the playground

to hang out and be with my friends.

I love and accept myself.

BC .4.

Even though

I know

after being bullied at school,

I am now scared and afraid

of being hit and hurt again,

and I just want to stay home.

I love and accept myself.

BC .5.

Even though

I know

after being roughed up and bullied,

I am now afraid to leave home,

go to school, or anywhere else,

in case it happens to me again.

I love and accept myself.

BC .6.

Even though

I know

that after being bullied,

I don't feel safe enough

to speak up, express myself,

or continue with my *……. classes anymore.

I love and accept myself

***Insert (dancing, acting, singing, music, drama, sports, etc.)**

Targeted EFT Statements

Bullying and Racism (BR)

This category covers various forms of harassment and abuse of children (and people) due to their ethnicity, skin colour, speech, clothes, cultural practices, food, customs, or religious practices.

Bullying and racism is often learned from the parents' views and comments from within the home, or their workplace and community, or from other children they are exposed to.

The Tapping statements are presented in the exact phrasing I recommend the facilitator use—spoken line by line for the child to repeat after each line during the session. This is done to prevent overwhelming an already stressed child.

Bullying Racism (BR)

BR .1.

Even though
**I feel
teased, abused, scared,
rejected and bullied,
by people and kids
due to the colour of my skin,
my clothes, customs, and religion.**
I love and accept myself.

BR .2.

Even though

I know

due to my race and culture,

I look different from most other kids,

and I isolate myself

and fit in where I can.

I love and accept myself.

BR .3.

Even though

I feel

sad, lonely, isolated,

rejected, and depressed

when kids say cruel,

and racially abusive comments

about me, my family,

my culture, and religion.

I love and accept myself.

BR .4.

Even though

I feel

that after being racially abused

and teased again,

I struggle to see how things

can get better and safer,

for me, my family, and my future.

I love and accept myself.

Bullying LGBTQIA+ (BL)

This category includes harassment and abuse based on actual or perceived sexual identity, or beliefs, including insults, exclusion, rumors, and intimidation, often leaving children feeling isolated, ashamed, anxious, and depressed.

The Tapping statements are presented in the exact phrasing I recommend the facilitator use—spoken line by line for the child to repeat after each line during the session. This is done to prevent overwhelming an already stressed child.

Bullying LGBTQIA+ (BL)

BL .1.

Even though

I feel

unsafe, nervous, judged, and abused

for how I look, speak and am.

I love and accept myself.

BL .2.

Even though

I know

after being abused

and beaten up at school again,

I feel scared and depressed,

and I struggle to see how things

can ever get safer and better for me.

I love and accept myself.

BL .3.

Even though

I know

I isolate myself

because I don't feel safe

and trust anyone.

I love and accept myself.

BL .4.

Even though

I feel

nervous and afraid to go to school

because I get picked on,

teased, abused, and hit by kids.

I love and accept myself.

BL .5.

Even though

I feel

angry and disrespected

when people force

their opinions and views on me.

I love and accept myself.

Bullying and Disability (BD)

This category includes bullying of children and people with disabilities, which can involve behaviors like mocking, exclusion, harm, or mistreatment. Often leading to them feeling angry, frustrated, shamed, and distressed. It is important to respond with understanding and care, as these children may already be carrying a great deal of physical, mental, and psychological stress.

The Tapping statements are presented in the exact phrasing I recommend the facilitator use—spoken line by line for the child to repeat after each line during the session. This is done to prevent overwhelming an already stressed child.

Bullying Disability (BD)

BD .1.

Even though

I feel

tense, angry, stressed and frustrated

when kids are not considerate and careful

of my disability, issues, needs, and support.

I love and accept myself.

BD .2.

Even though

I feel

sad, angry, and frustrated

when kids tease, mock,

and make fun of me.

I love and accept myself.

BD .3.

Even though

I feel

sad, stressed, rejected, and invisible

when kids don't talk to me,

share, and include me.

I love and accept myself.

BD .4.

Even though

I know

I have good days and bad days

that makes things frustrating for me,

my carers, friends, classmates, and others.

I love and accept myself.

BD .5.

Even though

I know

I get angry and frustrated with myself

when I am slow answering a question.

I love and accept myself.

BD .6.

Even though

I know

that there are times

when I don't love or like how I am,

and I just feel sad, stuck, and depressed.

I love and accept myself.

Bullying Actions (BA)

This category is for times when a child displays bullying behavior. This can happen when a child becomes impatient, anxious, frustrated, or feels they are missing out. These feelings can lead them to become angry, mean, controlling, and dismissive of other children's feelings, needs and situations.

Some bullying behavior may stem from how a child has been treated in their own home, leading them to adopt bullying as a coping mechanism, to get their needs met. They may target unsuspecting, vulnerable children and attempt to pressure, manipulate, or overwhelm them to achieve their desired outcome.

The Tapping statements are presented in the exact phrasing I recommend the facilitator use—spoken line by line for the child to repeat after each line during the session. This is done to prevent overwhelming an already stressed child.

Bullying Actions (BA)

BA .1.

Even though

I feel

angry, annoyed, and frustrated

when kids are too slow

and I have to wait my turn.

I love and accept myself.

BA .2.

Even though

I feel

angry and jealous

when I see other kids

getting everything they want,

and I never do.

I love and accept myself.

BA .3.

Even though

I know

I say mean and hurtful things

to get what I want,

because that

is what has happened to me.

I love and accept myself.

BA .4.

Even though

I feel

sad and angry

when I am called a bully.

When all I wanted,

was for things to be fair.

I love and accept myself.

Abuse and Violation (AV)

All children have a need for their personal space and physical boundaries to be respected in their home and lives. When someone abuses a child, it can leave the child feeling shocked, disrespected, violated, and afraid for their safety.

These statements cover the sexualization of children, including sexual objectification, sexual abuse, and violation. This includes exposing children to inappropriate sexual stories, comments, and images.

The Tapping statements are presented in the exact phrasing I recommend the facilitator use—spoken line by line for the child to repeat after each line during the session. This is done to prevent overwhelming an already stressed child.

Abuse and Violation (AV)

AV .1.

Even though
I feel
tense, stressed, and afraid
when people get too close to me,
and try to touch me.
I love and accept myself.

AV .2.

Even though

I feel

nervous, angry and abused

when I get looked at, touched, and felt up

by people I know or strangers.

I love and accept myself.

AV .3.

Even though

I feel

scared, nervous and angry

when people are fake and pretend

to be friendly and safe in public,

but touch and abuse me in private.

I love and accept myself.

AV .4.

Even though

I feel

scared, tense, and nervous

when boys and men stare,

smile and talk to me,

and try to get my attention.

I love and accept myself.

AV .5.

Even though

I feel

stressed, nervous, and anxious,

after what happened to me,

and I have trouble trusting

and speaking to anyone.

I love and accept myself.

AV .6.

Even though

I feel

nervous, tense, and unsafe,

since that bad experience,

and I now have trouble resting and sleeping.

I love and accept myself

AV .7.

Even though

I fear

after what happened to me,

that bad things will happen to me again.

I love and accept myself.

AV .8.

Even though

I fear

I may never feel safe enough to trust,

talk to, or be close to anyone again.

I love and accept myself.

AV .9.

Even though

I feel

upset, unsafe, disturbed, and shocked

after what was done to me,

and from what I saw and heard.

I love and accept myself.

Overwhelm and Depression (OD)

When a child experiences a challenging situation that they are not mentally prepared for or are unable to cope with and understand, their mind may struggle to focus and process the information and the situation. In some cases, the child's mind may freeze, go into shock, numb out, and dissociate, leaving the child feeling confused, shocked, overwhelmed, and depressed.

The Tapping statements are presented in the exact phrasing I recommend the facilitator use—spoken line by line for the child to repeat after each line during the session. This is done to prevent overwhelming an already stressed child.

Overwhelm and Depression (OD)

OD .1.

Even though

I know

that my mind gets distracted,

and I struggle to concentrate

and pay attention in class.

I love and accept myself.

OD .2.

Even though

I feel

stressed, unsure, afraid, and confused

about what I should do now to help myself.

I love and accept myself.

OD .3.

Even though

I feel

nervous, sad, stressed, and depressed

when I think about my Mom, Dad,

and family situation.

I love and accept myself.

OD .4.

Even though

I feel

stressed, confused, and frustrated

when my head is full of thoughts and worries.

I love and accept myself.

OD .5.

Even though

I feel

I don't have any real friends,

which leaves me feeling sad,

lonely, isolated, and depressed.

I love and accept myself.

Completion Statements (CS)

Once the Tapping statements have been tapped through, we need to reinforce the positive changes by selecting the appropriate Completion statements.

These statements help the child to feel happier and have new, positive perspectives about their life.

The Completion statements are presented in the exact phrasing I recommend the facilitator use—spoken line by line for the child to repeat after each line during the session. This is done to prevent overwhelming an already stressed child.

Completion Statements (CS)

CS .1.

I know that I can now speak up
and ask for help from Mom or Dad
whenever I need it.

CS .2.

I know that it may take time
for me to recover from this
and that is okay.

CS .3.

I am now ready
to learn, talk, share, play,
and be with other kids again.

CS .4.

I feel calm and balanced,
and I am ready to learn, speak up,
and go back to school now.

CS .5.

I feel okay with who I am
and how I am now.

CS .6.

I know that some kids at school
look and are different to me,
and I'm ok with that.

CS .7.

I am now ready to be seen
for whom I am,
have friends and enjoy my life.

CS .8.

I feel thankful
for the teachers and people,
who listen and care for me
and help me get through difficult times.

CS .9.

I know today is a good day
for me to start again.

Modifying Tapping Statements

Sometimes you may find that you need to slightly modify the words in a Tapping statement to fit the specific need of the child you are working with. Some statements refer to mom, dad, brother, and sister.

For example, if the child has only one parent, their mom, or whomever is the primary caregiver, you can modify the Tapping statement to suit that situation.

In place of titles or names, you can also use terms like 'the boy,' 'the boys,' 'the man,' 'the men,' 'the girl,' 'the girls,' 'the woman,' 'others,' etc., to suit the situation when the names are unknown.

Example 1 of Modifying a Tapping Statement

Parents, Siblings and Family

PSF .1. Original

Even though

I feel

sad, unloved and unimportant

when Mom and Dad

are too busy working

to spend time with me.

I love and accept myself.

PSF .1. Modified

Even though

I feel

sad, unloved and unimportant

when <u>Mom is</u> too busy working

to spend time with me.

I love and accept myself.

If the child is having a problem with a known person, then that person's name can be used in the Tapping statement. When we are stressed, angry, or hurt by someone, our mind often fixates on that person to an unhealthy degree.

Example 2 of Modifying a Tapping Statement

Bullying and Conflict

BC .2. Original

Even though

I feel

scared, judged, angry,

frustrated, and powerless

when kids tease, mock, and bully me.

I love and accept myself.

BC .2. Modified

Even though

I feel

scared, judged, angry,

frustrated, and powerless

when <u>Jessy, Anna, and Jaz</u>

tease, mock, and bully me.

I love and accept myself.

Use your discretion at this point, as it is important to keep the Tapping process simple and clear for both the child and you, as the facilitator.

Example of Choosing Tapping Statements for a Child Experiencing Stress

Seven-year-old Ash felt scared, hurt, sad, and stressed because Gemma bullied her at school. Gemma pushed Ash around and demanded her lunch money. Out of fear of being hurt, Ash gave Gemma her lunch money.

A week later, Ash is still upset by the incident and is afraid to go out and play with other children in the schoolyard. Ash is afraid of being confronted by Gemma again, and Ash chooses to sit in the library during lunch breaks.

The importance of choosing three Tapping statements with Targeted EFT is we are delivering a layered approach to de-stress Ash's mind, to take it out of shock and overwhelm and help return it to a healthy balance as quickly and effectively as possible.

Let us take a closer look at selecting each statement and the importance of the order.

Selecting Tapping Statement One

The first tapping statement you select should represent how the child feels about the stressful event in this moment now.

This is because a week or so may have passed between the child experiencing the incident and the Targeted EFT session being arranged. In our example, during this time, Ash may have moved on in many ways, wishing it never happened, and may not want to talk or think about it anymore.

However, Ash's parents, teachers, and school friends may have shared their opinions and comments about what they think happened, and how Ash should have reacted. This can either reinforce the Ash's perspective or create confusion for her about what she could do next.

Additionally, Ash's mind will have formed its own perspective of the situation, which could involve feelings of hurt, victimization, abuse, disrespect, fear, anxiety, and overwhelm leading to feelings of depression. All of this can influence how Ash feels by the time the Tapping session takes place.

1st Tapping Statement in the category of 'Rejected and Abandonment' (RA) RA .1.

Even though
I feel
scared, nervous, sad and lonely.
I love and accept myself.

Selecting Tapping Statement Two

The second statement you select can be more specific about the issues based on the information you have gathered from Ash.

2nd Tapping Statement in the category of 'Overwhelm and Depression' (OD) OD .2.

Even though
**I feel
stressed, unsure, afraid, and confused
about what I should do now
to help myself.**
I love and accept myself.

Selecting Tapping Statement Three

The third statement you select will either be based upon Ash's response or continue the theme of the second statement.

3rd Tapping Statement in the category of 'Bullying and Conflict' (BC) BC .3.

Even though
**I know
after being picked on and bullied at school
I am now afraid to go to the playground
and talk to and be with my friends.**
I love and accept myself.

Once you have tapped through that statement, ask Ash how they are feeling. If she is still feeling nervous, anxious or upset, select the next most relevant statement to best reflect her response about how she feels now.

If Ash says she is feeling calmer and okay, you can move to the Completion Tapping statement part of the Tapping process. Usually by three or four Tapping statements the child would be feeling better.

Selecting Completion Statements

To complete the Tapping process, select one or two Completion statements (CS) from the nine options available, to help Ash anchor the changes made by the previous Tapping statements. For Ash, I would select the following Completion statements.

1st Completion Statement (CS):

CS .1.

**I know
that I can speak up
and ask for help now
whenever I need it.**

2nd Completion Statement (CS):

CS .2.

**I feel calm and balanced,
and ready to learn, speak up,
and go back to school now.**

This example gives you an idea of how to select the most effective Tapping statements for a child's situation.

9

LEARNING TO FACILITATE AND PRACTICE THE TARGETED EFT PROCESS

Before guiding a child through a Targeted EFT session, it is important that you, the facilitator, feel confident and well-prepared.

To begin learning to become a Targeted EFT facilitator follow these practical steps.

1. Watch the Tutorial Videos

Start by watching the Targeted EFT tutorial videos, to get a clear overview of the full process. Follow along with me and experience the Targeted EFT process firsthand as you are guided through each step.
Go to https://www.helpingkidsriseandshine.com/videos/tutorials.

2. Print Out Guides and Tapping Statements

Print out **The Targeted EFT Tapping Sequence Guide**, which summarizes the key instruction. There is a version for both home and school use. Also print out **The Tapping Statements for Children**.

If possible, put these pages into clear plastic sleeves for their protection and durability and place them in a folder as you will be needing it for every Targeted EFT session you facilitate.
Go to https://www.helpingkidsriseandshine.com/resources.

3. Practice the Tapping Process

After watching the tutorial videos, practice the process a few times on your own, if possible, in front of a large mirror e.g. bathroom mirror. This helps you to become comfortable with sharing the Tapping process with another person.

With each practice session, you will begin to develop confidence and a natural rhythm for delivering a Targeted EFT session.

While these Tapping statements are specifically written for children, they can benefit the adults who take the time to tap them through on themselves.

As a therapist, I have noticed that some adults—including myself at times—are really just grown-up children who have learned to cope and adapt from the challenges they experienced in their own childhood and family life. ☺

These issues, which I refer to as originating from our wounded inner child and wounded inner teenager, may still be active in an adult's mind. They can sabotage the adult's ability to give and receive in balance, speak up for their needs and wishes, share, love, and communicate well in their relationships and encounters, including their ability to function well in their life.

4. Practice With a Willing Adult

When you're ready, invite a willing adult to participate in a practice session. Use the opportunity to go through the full facilitator process. This will help you become familiar with the questioning technique and help you to feel comfortable selecting the best Tapping statements from the options available.

In your role-play session, practice each of these important steps:

1. Have your folder with the printed out **The Targeted EFT Tapping Sequence Guide** and the **Tapping Statements for Children** ready to use.

2. Obtain the person's consent for a Tapping session

3. Set up a quiet, comfortable space and arrange seating

4. Gather information about a recent or past stressful incident

5. Ask supportive, clarifying questions to deepen your understanding of their issues

6. Select the most appropriate Tapping statements

7. Guide them through the Targeted EFT process.

With this foundational training in place, you are now ready to see how a full Targeted EFT session unfolds with a child.

In the next chapter, you will be guided through the step-by-step process for both home and school Tapping sessions.

The structure outlined in Chapter 10 is designed to help you apply what you have learned and practiced.

What May Happen When Facilitating a Tapping Session with a Child

As a facilitator, the children you work with may respond or react in different ways to the Tapping process and Tapping statements you are presenting to them. Remember everything is new to them—you, repeating Tapping statements, following instructions for tapping, counting, and humming. Be clear, calm, and sensitive as you explain the process to them.

When a child hears you read out a Tapping statement, they may become sad and emotional if it reminds them of the hurtful, stressful situation they have experienced, which causes them to stop talking, gasp, tear up, or cry etc.

Reactions from the child need to be gently managed as they confirm that the Tapping statement reflects the issues they are affected by. At such times, the facilitator is encouraged to reassure the child that they are safe, and ask them to please breathe, focus, and continue to say the words and follow the instructions.

This is actually the intention of the Tapping statement—to momentarily activate those hurtful memories. Just like a spark plug in an engine, its activation creates a reaction.

The important thing to realize here is that this spark of acknowledgement from within the child's mind is only a momentary reaction. It provides just enough energy for the Tapping process to access and transform the issue, then guide the child's mind to a new, safer, calmer, more comfortable place within itself.

What to Expect at the Conclusion of a Tapping Session with a Child

At the completion of a Targeted EFT Tapping session, most children will feel happier, calmer, and more settled within themselves. It is important to appreciate that any improvement in how the child feels is progress, and we can be grateful for helping to create those positive changes for them.

When necessary, additional Tapping sessions can be arranged to help children manage, improve, and strengthen their ability to cope better in both their home and school lives.

Targeted EFT Is Scalable

With experience, confident facilitators can guide the Targeted EFT process not only for a single child, but also for a small group, a classroom, or even an entire school assembly—highlighting its versatility and effectiveness.

In situations that may impact many, such as a school-wide or community shock or tragedy, Targeted EFT offers a way to support hundreds of children as they process what has happened, calm their emotions, recenter themselves, and begin to recover.

10

PREPARING FOR AND FACILITATING TARGETED EFT SESSIONS

Well done for making it this far—you are now ready to work with a child in a Targeted EFT session.

Many of the requirements for the facilitator are the same once the initial details have been attended to as to whether this is a Home or School based Tapping Session. There are downloadable Facilitator Check lists to help prepare for each type of session. The link to these is provided in the **Resources** section.

The specific differences are outlined as *Part 1a: Home-Based Tapping* and *Part 1b: School-Based Tapping*.

PART 1A: HOME-BASED TAPPING

Arranging a Tapping Session at Home for a Child

In a home setting, a Tapping session can offer a child comfort and familiarity as they begin to address a stressful experience. Typically, the child will have already shared information about the experience with their parent(s). If a parent—or another trusted, caring adult—has learned to facilitate the Targeted EFT process, they can proceed with facilitating the Tapping session as outlined.

When the facilitator is not the parent, it is suggested that the parent(s) sits in the room behind the child, out of their direct line of sight, during the Tapping session. This can help the child feel safe and secure during the session.

Arranging for a Targeted EFT Facilitator to Work with a Child and Their Parents in the Home

When choosing a Targeted EFT facilitator, it is important for the parent(s) to interview them to determine whether they feel confident in the facilitator's ability to help their child with their issues i.e., bullying, harassment, anxiety, or abuse etc. The parents can discuss their child's experiences in general terms and ask whether the facilitator has worked successfully with children facing similar challenges.

The parents should also ask whether the facilitator holds a current 'Blue Card' (or equivalent form of identification for working with children) and request to see it before the Tapping session begins. (As mentioned in Chapter 6: Facilitator's Role and Responsibilities).

Once the parents have agreed to work with the facilitator, they can provide more of the background information about the child's issues to help the facilitator prepare appropriately for the Tapping session.

On the day of a session, it is important for the parent(s) to check in with the child to ensure that they feel comfortable and are still willing to proceed with the session. If the child has changed their mind, the facilitator should be advised immediately, especially if they are travelling a significant distance to get to the appointment.

If the child agrees to the Tapping session with the facilitator, the parent(s) can reassure them that they will be safe and in the room with them.

When the facilitator arrives, the parent(s) can introduce them to the child. The facilitator will then explain how the table and chairs should be set up for the session.

Once everybody is seated, the facilitator will begin by gathering information from the child about what happened to them as outlined in **Part 2: Gathering Information and Selecting the Tapping Statements**, on page 142.

PART 1B: SCHOOL-BASED TAPPING

How to Guide a Tapping Session at School with a Child

In a school situation, if a child reports to a teacher that they have been hurt, abused, or bullied etc., the teacher will likely need to complete an incident report that officially records the child's complaint. As well as arrange for any first aid and other requirements for discipline that may need to be followed through with.

After this, if the decision is made that the child could benefit from a Tapping session, the next step is for the facilitator to contact the custodial parent to ask whether they agree to their child receiving a Tapping session and to provide their consent by signing a Consent Form.

Once the consent has been received, the facilitator can schedule the Targeted EFT session, and obtain a copy of the incident report. It might take a few days for the facilitator to arrange all preparations and be ready to facilitate the Tapping session with the child and their parent(s).

On the day of a Tapping session, it is important for the parent(s) to check in with the child to ensure that they feel comfortable and willing to proceed with the session. The parent(s) should reassure the child that they are safe, and that anything they share will be treated with care and that they will stay in the room with them.

Once the child agrees, the parent(s) can introduce the child to the school's facilitator. The parent(s) then shares with the facilitator any other relevant information about the child's situation, as outlined in **Part 2: Gathering Information and Selecting the Tapping Statements**, on page 142.

PART 2: GATHERING INFORMATION AND SELECTING THE TAPPING STATEMENTS

It is important to start the gathering information by asking the child how they are feeling now about what happened, using their own words to describe the experience.

Some children may need gentle encouragement and questioning from you to help you fully understand what happened and how they are feeling. Be sensitive and empathetic when speaking to the child. If you are unfamiliar to them, they may naturally feel cautious.

The facilitator can ask the parent if the child has forgotten to mention any important details about their experience. At this point, the facilitator may refer to the **List of Possible Questions to Ask the Child** below.

As the child shares, write down any key words they use as this will help you to choose the most appropriate Tapping statements to support them.

The facilitator may ask the parent if the child is displaying any stress-related changes. Such as disturbed sleep, bed-wetting, anger or tearful outburst, withdrawal, or other changes in their behavior. These responses can be unconscious reactions to the stress, tension, fear, or trauma they have experienced.

List of Possible Questions to Ask the Child

You could start with asking this question:

"I understand something upsetting happened to you, (insert their name). Would you like to tell me about it, please?" You might respond, for example, by saying, *"Oh, that wasn't very nice."*

Continue with a few of these types of questions if applicable:

- *"Were any nasty or scary things said to you?"*

- *"Were you hit or hurt?"*

- *"Was anything taken from you, like money, your phone, lunch, possessions, or your school bag?"*

- *"Do you know who they were?"*

- *"How many other kids were there?"*

- *"Did they threaten you or ask you to do anything?"*

- *"Have you seen them since?"*

- *"Have they said anything else to you since then?"*

- *"Who have you told about this?"*

- *"Did you tell your parents or your teacher?"*

- *"Is there anything else you would like to share about that?"*

- *"How have you felt since then?"*

- *"Have you been sleeping well? Have you had any bad dreams?"*

- *"How does all of that make you feel now?"*

If these questions have the child feeling sad, upset, and reluctant to talk about these topics, gently remind them that they are safe. Encourage them to take a deep breath and maybe have a sip of water, then invite them to continue sharing what happened.

Thank them for sharing that information. Reassure the child that they are safe, and ask them to take a few slow, deep breaths in and out to help them stay calm.

Next, select three Tapping statements that best reflect the issues the child is impacted by and write down their alphanumeric codes.

Select Tapping Statements

Here is an example of Tapping statements that may be selected for a child's issues.

Code RA.1 stands for *Rejection and Abandonment*, Tapping Statement 1.
Code UA.1 stands for *Upset and Angry*, Tapping Statement 1.
Code BC.1 stands for *Bullying and Conflict*, Tapping Statement 1.

Position The Targeted EFT Tapping Sequence Guide

From *The Targeted EFT Tapping Sequence Guide* —position the pages for **Part 3: The Targeted EFT Tapping Sequence** so they are clearly visible to you. If you are using a tablet, you may need to write out the selected Tapping statements in full to make the next steps easier to follow.

PART 3: THE TARGETED EFT TAPPING SEQUENCE

Step 1: The Setup

The Tapping sequence starts with the **Setup**, where the **Karate Chop point** is tapped while the **selected Tapping statement** is read aloud.

This tells the child's mind we are about to engage with the stored memories related to the incident or stressful situation that they experienced.

1. Ask the child to take a slow, deep breath in and out.

2. Begin by gently tapping the Karate Chop Point (see diagram) on the side of your hand (either hand) with the index and middle fingers.

3. Read the first Tapping statement selected aloud slowly and clearly, a few words at a time.

    After each line you speak, ask the child to repeat those words back to you while gently tapping on the Karate Chop point, as you demonstrate.

Example 1: Rejection and Abandonment

RA.1.

(Diagram 1)

"Even though"

the child repeats this

"I feel"

the child repeats this

"scared, nervous"

the child repeats this

"sad and lonely."

the child repeats this

"I love and accept myself."

the child repeats this

4. **Repeat this step** so that the full statement is spoken and tapped through **twice**.
5. This completes Step 1: The Setup.

Targeted EFT Sessions

Step 2: The Tapping Sequence

This step only uses words of the statement that are in **bold print** that begin with words **"I feel"**, **"I know"**, or **"I fear"**.

Example 1: Rejection and Abandonment
RA.1.
(Diagram 2)

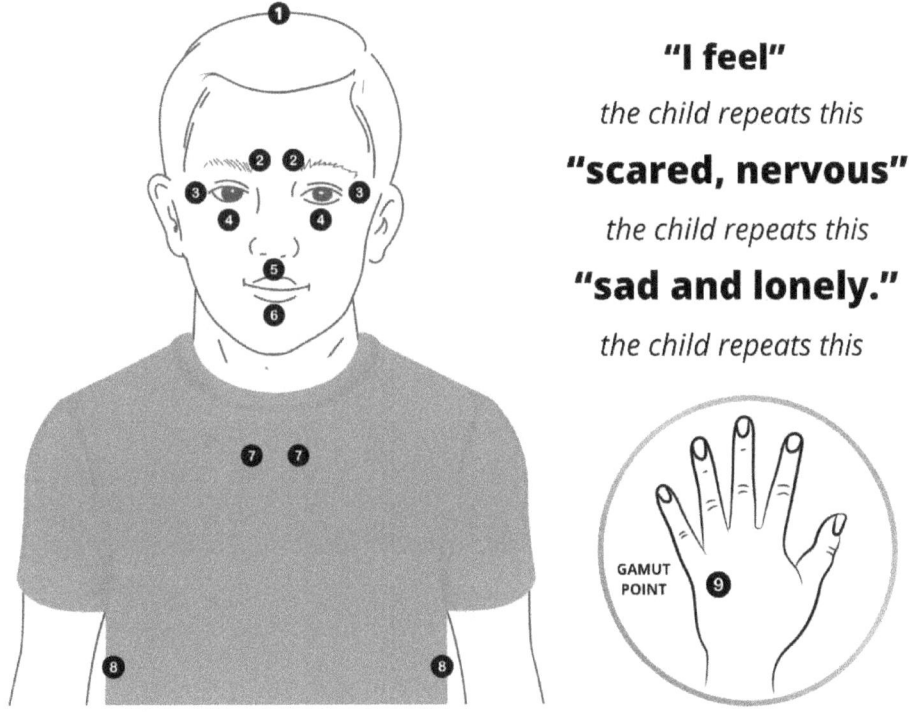

1. Ask the child to take a slow, deep breath in and out.
2. Then you read the words in **bold print** of the selected Tapping statement aloud —slowly and clearly—as shown.
3. After each line you speak, ask the child to repeat those words back to you while gently tapping the points 1 to 9 as you demonstrate. Repeat the words again, when needed, till you both finish tapping at the 9th point on the hand (the Gamut point).

Step 3: Eye Movements, Humming, and Counting

This step engages the mind with eye movements, humming, and counting. It can be fun, and children often love this part! It helps shift the focus of the child's mind by involving it in left and right brain activities.

1. Ask the child to take a slow, deep breath in and out.
2. Then ask the child to follow these instructions:

   (Diagram 3)

   a) *"Look straight ahead, close your eyes, open them again, still looking straight ahead."*

   b) *"Without moving your head, look down hard right (toward your right knee), then return to looking straight ahead."*

   c) *"Still keeping your head still, look down hard left, (toward your left knee), then return to looking straight ahead."*

   d) *"Roll your eyes in a full clockwise circle, then return to looking straight ahead."*

   e) *"Roll your eyes in a full counterclockwise circle, then return to looking straight ahead."*

3. Ask the child to take a slow, deep breath in and out.
4. Next, ask the child to hum the start of Happy Birthday.
   You hum "Happy Birthday to you", (just this bit) and they hum it back to you.
5. Next ask the child to count to 5. Then you say "1. 2. 3. 4. 5", and they count back to you.
6. And then ask the child to hum the start of Happy Birthday again.
   You hum "Happy Birthday to you" and they hum it back to you.

Targeted EFT Sessions

Step 4: Follow the Tapping Sequence Again

After involving the child's mind in the left and right brain activities, it is now receptive to the next step of calming and reducing the stress it has been holding about the issues and topics.

1. After each line you speak, ask the child to repeat those words back to you while gently tapping the points 1 to 9, as you demonstrate. Repeat the words again, when needed till you both finish tapping at the 9th point (the Gamut point).

Example 1: Rejection and Abandonment
RA.1.

(Diagram 2 repeated)

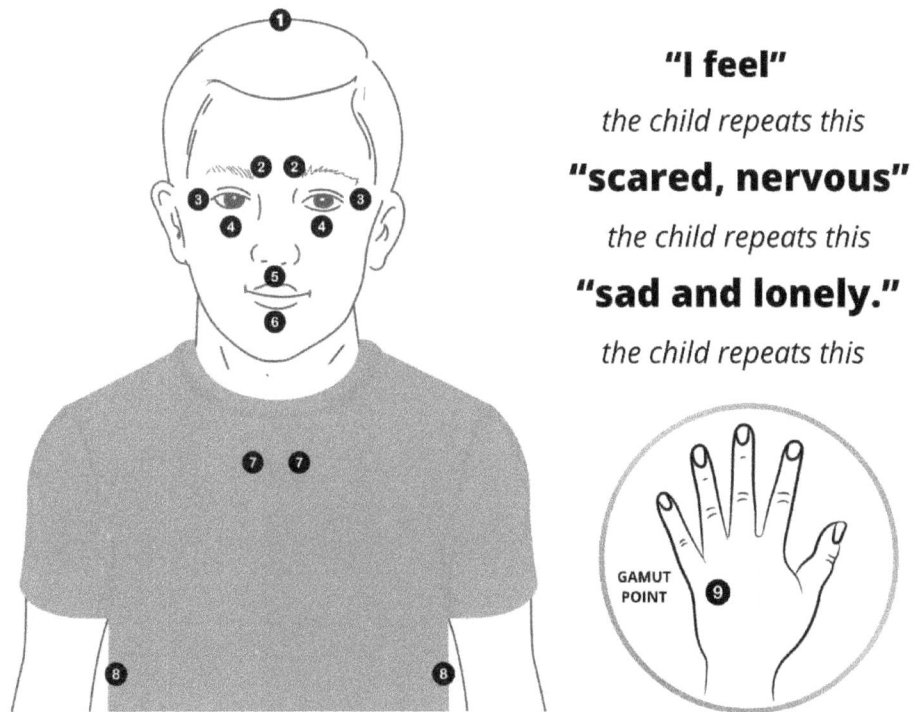

"I feel"
the child repeats this
"scared, nervous"
the child repeats this
"sad and lonely."
the child repeats this

Congratulations!
You've just completed the first Tapping statement.

Step 5: Repeat Steps 1 to 4 with the Next Tapping Statement

1. Begin **Step 1: The Setup**, with the next Tapping statement.

   Follow from Step 1 on page 145 and continue with Steps 2, 3, and 4 from the previous example.

2nd Tapping Statement

Example: Upset and Angry

UA.1.

(Diagram 4)

"Even though"

the child repeats this

"I feel"

the child repeats this

"stressed and angry"

the child repeats this

"when I get things wrong"

the child repeats this

"at school and home."

"I love and accept myself."

the child repeats this

2. **After the Third Tapping Statement is Tapped Through:** Check in with the child after completing that Tapping statement. If they are still stressed or upset, repeat Steps 1 to 4 with the next Tapping statement that you feel best suits their current feelings.

   If they seem more relaxed and happier within themselves, move on to **Step 6: Select Two Completion Statements to Finish Tapping Session.**

Step 6: Select Two Completion Statements to Finish Tapping Session

Select two of the most appropriate Completion statements to tap through to finish the Tapping session.

This step anchors the process and reinforces the benefits and positive changes you have made together—a co-creation of care and support for the child.

1. Ask the child to take a slow, deep breath in and out.
2. Read the statement aloud, slowly and clearly, a few words at a time. At the same time, gently tap point 9, the Gamut Point, as before. After each line you speak, ask the child to repeat those words back to you while gently tapping on point 9, as you demonstrate.

Example: Completion Statement
CS.1.
(Diagram 5)

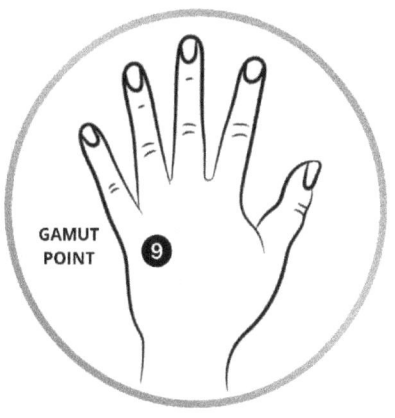

"I know"

the child repeats this

"that I can now speak up"

the child repeats this

"and ask for help from Mom or Dad"

the child repeats this

"whenever I need it."

the child repeats this

3. Repeat with the next Completion statement.

PART 4: CONCLUDING THE TAPPING SESSION

1. Ask the child how they are feeling now, they may seem more relaxed and maybe chatty. If they have more to say and share, then give them a few minutes to express this.
2. Thank the child and parent (or guardian) for joining with you in this process.
3. If possible, have their parent (or guardian) update you about how the child is feeling over the next two weeks, as they may need a follow up Tapping session.

FREQUENTLY ASKED QUESTIONS

Q: Is consent required before Tapping is used with a child?

A: Yes, a child, teenager, or adult must be willing and interested in taking part in the Targeted EFT process. If the parent is not the facilitator—such as in a school setting—I recommend that the custodial parent(s) or guardian(s) provide written consent for their child to participate in a Tapping session. The school may also have specific policies regarding delivering well-being processes like this. Additionally, be sure to follow any legal requirements that apply in your region, state, or country.

Q: What if the child changes their mind about taking part in a Tapping session?

A: Sometimes, a child may change their mind and become unavailable at the agreed time.

If the child's mood, stress levels, state of mind, or external—such as school, home, or family issues—are concerning them, then the Tapping session should be postponed until the child feels ready, willing, and trusting enough to participate.

This is why I have included the **Facilitator's Intention Statement**—to remind you that you are only responsible for your role in the Tapping session. If the child is not ready to follow through on the day, parents must respect their decision and advise the facilitator if and when they do feel ready to participate in a Tapping session, understanding that this time may never come.

Q: During a Targeted EFT session with a child, are we recreating the issue or trauma by having them read a Tapping statement?

A: No.

As the facilitator of the Targeted EFT process, it is important to understand that the Tapping statements provided have been specifically worded to initiate a slight reaction and recognition from the child's mind.

We only need the child's mind to momentarily recognize the memory of the issue or trauma for the Tapping process to access and begin reducing the impact of the issues the child is stressed by. This may relate to a current issue or event, a past memory the child's mind has stored, or, in some cases, something the child's mind believes has happened, or fears might happen to them.

Q: Why do some of the words presented in the Tapping statements appear to be sad and negative?

A: The Targeted EFT Tapping statements are specifically worded to reflect the thoughts of the conscious survival-focused mind, which can include negative comments and thoughts. While this part of the mind ultimately wants the best for the child, it often uses negative words and feelings in an attempt to control or protect them.

Q: What if in a Tapping session the child becomes upset or cries?

A: Offer them a tissue. Participating in the Targeted EFT process may be a new experience for the child, and they might feel nervous, embarrassed, or unsure about speaking up and expressing their emotions. Tears can be a healthy emotional release and are part of the natural process of emotional rebalancing. In these moments, the facilitator's role is to gently comfort the child, reassure them that they are safe, and encourage them to continue with the Tapping process.

Frequently Asked Questions

Q: Can I use Zones of Regulation® to help me identify how a child is feeling before and after a Tapping session?

A: Yes. Zones of Regulation®[41] is a great tool and resource for teachers or parents to use to help them identify how a child is feeling. This can be very helpful for identifying the appropriate Tapping statements to choose, which are categorized by issue and /or emotional state. If the child is already used to using the Zones of Regulation® tools, they may find the Tapping process easier to understand and participate more willingly.

Q: How is Tapping different to other well-being tools like Mindfulness?

A: Mindfulness is a well-being tool that is increasingly being incorporated into schools worldwide to help children manage stress, reduce anxiety, and improve focus—with proven benefits.

While mindfulness is effective in promoting a calm and focused state, Targeted EFT, as the name suggests, offers a targeted approach to reducing the stress a child feels from the negative issues and experiences they have been impacted by. This makes Targeted EFT a highly effective tool for realigning and supporting the emotional well-being of children both at home and in schools.

Q: Can a person who learns the Targeted EFT process from this book charge a fee to facilitate a Targeted EFT session for a child?

A: This book provides information to help parents, teachers, or caring adults learn how to facilitate a Targeted EFT session for a child. The person who learns this process and offers their services may choose to charge a fee, which could cover

---

[41] Aussie Childcare Network. (2023, November 21). *The Zones of Regulation*. https://aussiechildcarenetwork.com.au/articles/teaching-children/zones-of-regulation

their time and travel expenses. The amount of the fee, if any, should be agreed upon between the facilitator and the parent(s) of the child they are helping.

We will soon be offering certified training courses in Targeted EFT, which will include how to deliver sessions for children, teenagers, and adults. Graduates will be eligible to charge for their services as Certified Facilitators of Targeted EFT.

These FAQs will be expanded upon and continuously updated on our website.
View at https://www.helpingkidsriseandshine.com/faqs

RESOURCES

The following resources are available for downloading, printing, and, in some cases, modification to suit your specific needs. To access them, type this web address into your browser exactly as shown: https://www.helpingkidsriseandshine.com/resources

Essential Documents for a Tapping Session with a Child

Home Use

1. Facilitator Check List for a Home-based Tapping Session

2. The Targeted EFT Tapping Sequence Guide (includes steps for delivering the Tapping process)

3. The Tapping Statements for Children

4. List of Possible Questions to Ask the Child

School Use

1. Facilitator Check List for a School-based Tapping Session

2. The Targeted EFT Tapping Sequence Guide

3. The Tapping Statements for Children

4. List of Possible Questions to Ask the Child

5. Benefits of a Targeted EFT Session for your Child (flyer)

The following documents are samples that are available to be modified to suit the requirement of your school:

6. Tapping Session Form for a School-based Facilitator

7. Tapping Session Request Email to a Parent/Guardian

8. Parental Consent Form

9. Waiver and Release of Liability Form

Tapping Video Links

To assist with facilitator training view the tutorial videos with Paul Boulton. Type this web address into your browser exactly as shown: https://www.helpingkidsriseandshine.com/videos/tutorials

Further Reading

While these sections contain valuable insights, we felt they would be better accessed as articles to preserve the book's overall flow. You can read them on our website. Go to https://www.helpingkidsriseandshine.com/articles

1. Stress Relief at Your Fingertips: EFT and Tapping Solutions

2. The EFT Tapping Points Explained

3. Erin's Law: Advocating for Sexual Abuse Education in Schools in the USA and Globally

REPORTING CONCERNS: ABUSE, BULLYING, OR CYBERBULLYING

If a child is in immediate danger, please call the police without delay.

Concerns about a child experiencing or having experienced sexual abuse, violation trauma, bullying, or cyberbullying can, in most cases, be reported anonymously.

For readers in countries not listed below, please check with your local police or appropriate child protection authorities.

Australia

- **Crime Stoppers:** www.crimestoppers.com.au

- **National Domestic Family and Sexual Violence Counselling Service:** 1800-RESPECT (1800 737 732) – available 24/7, www.1800respect.org.au

- **Kids Helpline:** For children and young people, 1800 55 1800 – available 24/7, www.kidshelpline.com.au

- **eSafety Commissioner:** For cyberbullying and online safety concerns, www.esafety.gov.au

New Zealand

- **Oranga Tamariki – Ministry for Children:** Freephone 0508 326 459, www.orangatamariki.govt.nz

- **Shine (Domestic violence support):** 0508 744 633 – available 24/7, www.2shine.org.nz

- **Youthline:** For young people experiencing bullying or emotional distress, 0800 376 633, www.youthline.co.nz

United States

- **Child Protection Services (CPS):** Check for details in your state.

- **Childhelp National Child Abuse Hotline:** 1-800-4-A-CHILD (1-800-422-4453) – available 24/7, www.childhelphotline.org

- **National Sexual Assault Hotline:** 1-800-656-HOPE (1-800-656-4673), www.rainn.org

- **StopBullying.gov:** For information and resources on bullying and cyberbullying, www.stopbullying.gov

United Kingdom

- **Children's Social Care:** Check for details via your local authority.

- **NSPCC (National Society for the Prevention of Cruelty to Children):** 0808 800 5000 – available 24/7, www.nspcc.org.uk

- **Childline:** For support with bullying and emotional distress, 0800 1111, www.childline.org.uk

ACKNOWLEDGMENTS

A heartfelt thank you to my partner, Elaine Gentles, whose unwavering love, support, empathy, and tech experience has been instrumental in bringing this project to life, especially through the editing and production phases. Your dedication and vision have been invaluable in shaping and refining this work with me.

I extend my gratitude to Kaye Menzies, Liz Wilkinson, Anita Parry, and Dr Fabien Mendoza, Chiropractor, for their contributions and insightful feedback. Also, to my children Kaia and Nat, who are a constant source of love and appreciation. To my family, friends, and clients, thank you for your support and encouragement.

A special thank you also goes to Aaron and Roger Ponton for their kindness and support.

I also give thanks to the Tapping and EFT pioneers, Dr. Roger Callahan and Gary Craig, respectively.

ABOUT THE AUTHOR

Paul Boulton is an intuitive therapist, author, and developer of Targeted Energy Focused Tapping, with over 20 years of experience helping clients worldwide lead more aware, empowered, and fulfilling lives. His clients have included CEOs, doctors, psychologists, nurses. defense personnel, teachers, actors, moms and dads, former nuns and priests, and people from all walks of life.

Based on the Sunshine Coast in Queensland, Australia, Paul has worked as a professional psychic for over 35 years. Paul combines his intuitive insight and empathic abilities, along with practical tools to help people create positive, lasting change in their lives. His goal is to provide insights that help clients gain the clarity and skills they need to make their best decisions and live their best life now.

In early 2003, Paul read *The EFT Manual* by Gary Craig, which he gifted to the world. The book detailed how Emotional Freedom Techniques™ had delivered great results for people who experienced stress, anxiety, trauma etc.

Soon after, Paul began developing his own, more therapy-focused version of tapping, which included him writing Tapping statements aimed specifically at the person's issues, he calls his version, Targeted Energy Focused Tapping (Targeted EFT).

Targeted EFT enables Paul to work with and support clients who have been challenged by relationship issues, divorce, abuse, bullying, violation, trauma, grief, depression, PTSD etc.

Paul uses Targeted EFT in conjunction with his psychic readings and offers this potent combination called a Positive Change Session, a highly effective approach that has benefited many of his clients.

Positive Change Sessions help people free their minds and emotions from the stuck fears, issues, abuse, and traumas they have experienced in their lives. These challenges may stem from difficulties in their childhood and family life, school, work, relationships, marriages, career, business and other situations.

Paul is passionate about his work and its potential to help adults, teenagers, and children recover from stress, anxiety, and challenges, allowing them to lead happier, more fulfilling lives.

"In my 40+ years of personal self-discovery, I have participated in numerous self-development courses, workshops, and seminars. While some of these workshops were effective and helpful, many lacked the depth of change, insights, and healing I had hoped for.

About the Author

This fueled my desire to create my own approach—a genuine, effective tapping process designed to help people grow beyond the challenges and hurts they have experienced.

Most people have had frights, shocks, abuse, rejection, and abandonment issues and trauma that has shaped their childhood, teenage and adult lives.

In response, their minds developed coping strategies to help them survive and get through their day.

This is why this book was written—to provide an effective, easy-to-follow resource for parents, teachers, and caring adults everywhere, to help stressed children begin to recover, heal, think, feel and function better in their lives."

— **Paul Boulton**

CONTACT US

Thank you for reading *Helping Kids Rise and Shine*! If you would like to connect, ask questions, or share your thoughts, we would love to hear from you. Whether you are reaching out with feedback, a personal story, or a simple hello—we welcome you.

Emails:
paul@paulboulton.com.au
hello@helpingkidsriseandshine.com

Websites:
www.paulboulton.com.au
www.helpingkidsriseandshine.com

Socials:
www.facebook.com/Paul Boulton
www.facebook.com/HelpingKidsRiseandShine
www.instagram.com/paulboulton.psychic.therapist
www.patreon.com/paulboulton

While *Helping Kids Rise and Shine* was written by me, Paul Boulton, bringing it to the world was very much a team effort. My partner, Elaine Gentles, managed the development, design, and publishing of all versions of the book. Together, we handle our marketing, sales, customer support, and communications—so you may receive a reply from either one of us.

With appreciation,
Paul & Elaine

www.ingramcontent.com/pod-product-compliance
Lightning Source LLC
Chambersburg PA
CBHW061157010526
44119CB00059B/848